the
hidden
code
of
cryptic
crosswords

This book is dedicated to Uncle Caspar who told me:
'Cryptic crossword clues are simply an encoded message, and
all one needs to do is to decode the message.'
This book explains the code.

the
hidden
code
of
cryptic
crosswords

francois greeff

foulsham

The Publishing House, Bennetts Close, Cippenham,
Slough, Berkshire, SL1 5AP, England

ISBN 0-572-02778-8

Printed in Great Britain by Creative Print and Design (Wales), Ebbw Vale

Contents

Introduction

" ...it remains an internationally recognised benchmark of intelligence, wit and a facility for lateral thinking... " James Fergusson, referring to the ability to complete *The Times* crossword in 'How to do *The Times* crossword,' *Mensa Quest*, April 1998, p16.

Why solve crossword puzzles?

How many of us eagerly look forward to the weekend newspapers and the chance to pit our wits against those devious-minded masters of the crossword? How many of us give up in disgust after a few hours of almost fruitless brainstorming, only to start all over again the following week? It is at these people that this book is mainly directed.

Crossword solving is a form of mental gymnastics and, as in physical gymnastics, there are certain rules and guidelines one should follow if one hopes to achieve any degree of competency in this sport. As with most things in life there are those individuals who appear to the rest of us to have a natural flair. This is true to a certain extent, but what we do not see when we watch the graceful gyrations of the world's finest, is the hours of practice and study of technique that go into the preparation for the final performance. I am not suggesting that the following pages provide a stringent training programme for the champion – on the contrary. The purpose of writing this book is to take the frustration out of crossword solving by providing a few basic techniques.

However, whether you are one of those who aspire to championship level, or whether you are just a weekend sportsman or woman wishing to improve your game, I believe that this book will be of great value to you.

How to use this book and gain value from it

Work backwards. Always start with the answer to a clue and consider it to be the problem. Work from the answer toward the question to figure out how the answer justifies the clue. This book was written because cryptic clues made no sense, not even when I had the answers to them. I once thought this clue (which recurs on page 29) to be typically nonsensical:

One before nine taking in a novice who is queuing up (2,1,4) = In a line

I learned the rules of the game by figuring out how the clues work from the answers instead of figuring out the answers from the clues. By finding out how clues work one learns the rules of this game, and only then can one begin to play it.

Secondly, accept that the slightest interest you may have in crosswords will require not that you know the meaning of every word that exists, but that you look it up immediately. In reading this book you must use the *Glossary*.

Thirdly, the shortest chapter in this book is just three pages long. It is the most important chapter in the whole book. If you read nothing but pages 10–12, *The Anatomy of Cryptic Clues*, you will already have done yourself a great service. The chapter is succinct and devoid of the 'hooptedoodle' that Mack deplores in Steinbeck's *Sweet Thursday*. The hooptedoodle is, as Mack suggests it should be, in a separate chapter all of its own. True to the nature of hooptedoodle, it restates what has been said in *The Anatomy of Cryptic Clues*, but says it with more detail, example, repetition and circumlocution. Mack also suggests that the hooptedoodle should be skipped over if you do not like it. But if you do read it you will find out why parts of the clues in this book are **bold**, <u>underlined</u>, in *italics,* or <u>double underlined</u>. If you forget the function of a font, go back to *Hooptedoodle (1)* or consult the *Key to fonts* on page 12. These altered fonts indicate the functions of words in the clues, as one might highlight the verbs in sentences or literary devices in poetry. Occasionally, I use capital letters to make something very obvious.

I have tried to use very many examples, since each one illustrates a point slightly differently. Each example reinforces the lesson and makes it easier to remember. Be sure to understand how the answer justifies the clue in each case. Examples have been taken from several sources, which have been acknowledged at the end of this book, but mainly from the WH Crossword and the Everyman's Crossword. I found them in the *Sunday Times Magazine* in Cape Town, but they have been syndicated and their origin lies in England. Those two puzzles were once an enigma to me, and they led to the writing of this book.

The navigation bar at the top of each page carries forward the structure of titles, sections and sub-sections that are still under discussion. The chapter title appears above the rule. The section or sections on the page appear beneath the rule. The sub-section heading appears in brackets.

Chapter Title

Section (Sub-section)

Finally, if you want to tell me anything, or ask something, please write to me at **goodgreeff@crossword-theory.com**. I welcome comments about this book and any ways you think it can be improved.

This book can be bought direct from the author at **www.hiddencode.co.uk** It makes a fine gift and is useful for wedging under doors to keep them open.

Francois Greeff
London

PART ONE

An Explanation of the Way Cryptic Crosswords Work

1. The Anatomy of Cryptic Clues

A cryptic clue is not a sentence, but has two distinct parts that must be separated. Every cryptic clue defines the answer twice: Once by a **synonym** ∧ *and once by wordplay.*

Bird ∧ *moves out of* <u>danger</u> (6) = Gander
Hero ∧ *stands among* <u>them, an</u>onymously (2-3) = He-man

The clue is made up of five parts:

1. The **synonymcrux** (in **bold**), because the crux of every clue lies in the synonym.

2. The fulcrum, ∧, separates the **synonymcrux** from the *wordplay*. It is the point at which the two separate definitions of the answer balance, and they, separately, have equal weight in each defining the answer.

3. The *keyword* (in *italics*) indicates the device used in the clue. That means that the keyword tells one 'what to do'.

4. The <u>exposition</u> (<u>underlined when letters move to the answer,</u> and <u>double underlined when another word is needed</u>) is the part of the clue that the device applies to; the part that 'what to do' is done to. For example:

Left ∧ <u>a wild pig</u> *in* <u>its own fat</u> (8) = Larboard

Becomes

Left ∧ <u>boar</u>   *in*   <u>lard</u>   (8) = Larboard (boar in lard)

5. The num is a pair of brackets containing numerals and is always the last part of the clue. The num defines the structure of the answer. For example, 'being two hyphenated words, one of two letters and the second of three letters' (he-man).

To sum up:

The clue is has five parts:		
1. **synonymcrux:**	**Bird**	**Hero**
2. fulcrum:	∧	∧
3. *keyword:*	*moves out of*	*stands among*
4. <u>exposition</u>:	<u>danger</u>	<u>them anonymously</u>
5. num:	(6)	(2-3)

Key to fonts (in this book)

Bold indicates the **synonymcrux** (See page 20).

Italics indicate *the keyword* (page 20).

~~Lines~~ indicate the exposition (page 23):

Underlining specifically indicates those parts of the exposition from which the answer is derived. Two kinds of underlining are used:

A single underline is used to indicate that the underlined letters are used in the answer.

A double underline is used to indicate the origin of an indirect path to the answer; i.e. that a synonym or paraphrase of the double underlined words is needed or that multiple devices are applied to the double underlined letters.

~~Lines struck-through letters~~ indicate parts of the exposition ~~not used~~ in the answer, and are used to further clarify letters which are used in the answer.

> A box surrounds important information which should not be skipped over.

The fulcrum mark, $\wedge$, separates the two definitions of the clue (page 24). The mark may be split in half so that it will contain a word or grapheme that acts as fulcrum in the clue. Generally this word is excluded from both definitions, but not always. Where a clue uses two fulcrum marks it shows that the part between them is common to both definitions.

Runs for $\wedge$ **100** $\wedge$ **years** (7) = Century
Runs for 100 = Century
100 years = Century

2. The Original Straight Clue

The mythical origin

When Jason sailed in the *Argo* to the land of the lotus-eaters he was sent in search of the golden fleece. His half-brother Pelias was sure that Jason would fail and wanted him to be killed. Instead, Jason returned with the fleece and killed Pelias. On his return to his home in Attica, one of his argonauts, Theseus, was to hoist a white sail as a signal of their success, but Theseus failed to do so. This led his father Aegeus to think that Theseus was dead. In his grief, the old man leaped into the sea and was drowned – thus jumping to a conclusion.

Meanwhile, the Greeks had their own troubles. King Minos of Crete, son of Zeus and Europa, had commissioned Daedalus to build a palace at Knossos. Daedalus – an architect, sculptor and inventor – was no fool. He built an excellent palace that included the legendary Labyrinth that housed a monster, half man, half bull: the Minotaur, that was fed on human flesh. When Daedalus was later imprisoned by Minos he made wings for himself and his son to escape, and they flew to Sicily. Sadly, only the father completed the flight. His son flew so close to the sun that it melted the wax which held the feathers in his wings. This caused young Icarus to fall into the sea and drown.

To feed the Minotaur, King Minos demanded of Athens an annual tribute of seven young men and seven maidens. Theseus asked to be included among them because he planned to kill the Minotaur. At Knossos, Ariadne, the daughter of King Minos and Pasiphaë, gave Theseus a clew of silken thread to aid him in the Labyrinth. He unwound the thread as he went into the Labyrinth, killed the Minotaur, then rewound the clew of thread to find his way out again. It is certain that if he had been clewless he would not have been able to solve the puzzle of the Labyrinth.

From this literal and metaphoric use of clew arose the further use of clew in the metaphoric sense. In time the word came to be spelled clue. Although clew may properly be used both metaphorically and literally, it is customary to use it only in the literal sense. Clue is never used literally as it is used exclusively to mean a suggestion of a train of thought to solve an intellectual problem (especially in solving crimes and crosswords). Today there are many types of crossword clue, all divisible into two main categories of crossword clues: straight and cryptic. We shall run through the types of straight clues quickly, to see later how they have survived in cryptic clues.

Straight clues

Straight clues are mostly ammels (where the meaning of a word is given and you have to find the word) or similar types such as genus and specie, general knowledge or paraphrase (by synonyms). There are other straight clue types which are used less often. The straight clue is typically short and direct. Before discussing the cryptic clue the straight clue must be understood perfectly. The following examples illustrate the common types.

GENUS AND SPECIE
The answer is exactly the same thing as the clue but is more specific.

Citadel (7) = Kremlin
Insects (7) = Beetles
Pasta (9) = Spaghetti
French composer (4) = Lalo
Rich red wine (6) = Claret

The exact opposite of this clue is where a specific example is given and the collective type is required in the answer. The clue is known as:

EXAMPLE AND TYPE
Sparrow (4) = Bird
Novel (4) = Book
Spade (4) = Tool
Spade (4) = Card
Spade (4) = Suit

GENERAL KNOWLEDGE
Either you know the answer or you don't. Consult a thesaurus or crossword list.

Scottish national emblem (7) = Thistle
Unit of force (4) = Dyne
Roman coin (2) = As
Mythological aeronaut (6) = Icarus
French composer (4) = Lalo

PARAPHRASE
To paraphrase is to express the same idea in other words. In these clues a synonym is called for.

Employ (3) = Use
Pleased (4) = Glad
Lobby (4) = Hall
Normal (5) = Usual
Rot (5) = Decay

AMMEL
An ammel is a dictionary entry given backwards. In other words, if one had the answer one could look it up and find the clue. They can be very frustrating, especially as with 'leat'.
Ill-bred person (5) = Churl
Irrational number (4) = Surd
Steep slope (5) = Scarp
Of the mouth (4) = Oral
Rise and fall (5) = Surge
Watercourse to a mill (4) = Leat

ABBREVIATION
In these examples it is interesting to note that some words, having already been abbreviated, require further abbreviation. Watch for answers requiring very few letters. The setter nonetheless saw fit to indicate that a two-letter answer required an abbreviation. These examples were all in a single puzzle and are copied exactly.

Straight clues (Abbreviation)

I owe you (3) = IOU
Umpire (abbr) (3) = Ump
It is (abbr) (3) = It's
Daniel (abbr) (3) = Dan
Ferrum (abbr) (2) = Fe
Bach Arts (2) = BA
Alt Curr (2) = AC
Ch Acct (2) = CA
O/draft (2) = OD
Lancs, England (2) = LE

Many are simply reduced to initial letters, a trick that is very often used in cryptic crosswords too.

Earl Marshall (2) = EM
Post dated (2) = PD
Red Cross (2) = RC
Anno Regni (2) = AR
Early English (2) = EE
Anno Dom (2) = AD
Save our souls (abbr) (3) = SOS
Los Angeles (2) = LA

PHRASE
Recognise and supply the missing bit.

Half . . . hour (2) = An
Head over . . . (5) = Heels
Good . . . gold (2) = As

NUMER
A numer is an alphabetic statement of a number; the use of letters instead of numeric figures.

Three (Roman) (3) = III
III (Roman) (5) = Three

Straight and cryptic clues compared

All the above types of clue also occur in cryptic crosswords, but they may be used concurrently or as devices in other types of clue. Consider these clues. (These examples are from crosswords that feature two sets of clues for the same set of answers: a set of straight clues and a set of cryptic clues. This is a useful and highly recommended way of learning how to solve cryptic crosswords.)

Straight:
Venomous creature (5) = Mamba
Cryptic:
Mother *takes* doctor a /\ **venomous creature** (5) = Mamba
Paraphrase mother and abbreviate doctor, 'a' stays 'a'
= Ma + MB (Bachelor of Medicine) + a

Straight:
Uncivilised (6) = Savage
Cryptic:
Uncivilised /\ *to set* sex appeal against maturity (6) = Savage
Abbreviate sex appeal and against, paraphrase maturity
= SA v (versus) Age
Straight:
Wine (6) = Claret
Cryptic:
Cartel *producing* /\ **wine** (6)= Claret
Genus and specie, confirmed by an anagram (rearrange letters to make new word) of cartel

Straight:
Plant (6) = Clover
Cryptic:
150 finished /in\ **plant** (6) = Clover
Numer restated in letters, paraphrase of finish
CL + over

Straight clues and cryptic clues compared

Straight:

Theatre publicity man (5,5) = Press agent

Cryptic:

<u>Urge</u> a <u>chap</u> /to become\ **theatre publicity man** (5,5) = Press agent

Paraphrase urge and chap, 'a' stays 'a'. The clue requires some general knowledge, and the recognisable phrase in the answer also helps.

Press a gent

Straight:

Intelligent (6) = Brainy

Cryptic:

Intelligent /\ <u>female supporter</u> <u>one</u> *takes to* <u>New York</u> (6) = Brainy

Paraphrase <u>female supporter</u>, express <u>one</u> in other letters (or as a figure that resembles a letter) and abbreviate <u>New York</u>

Bra + I + NY

Straight:

Strength (5) = Brawn

Cryptic:

Strength /of\ <u>potted meat</u> (5) = Brawn

Potted meat is an ammel, to be found by looking up 'brawn' in a dictionary. Alternatively, paraphrase potted meat.

These examples illustrate how the straight clue is always repeated in the cryptic clue. This fact must never be forgotten. **The straight clue is always somewhere in the cryptic clue – always, without exception.** What is even more important is that **the little straight clue is always at the end of the cryptic clue; either the front end or the back end – never in the middle.** There is absolutely nothing that one can learn about cryptic crosswords that is more useful or more important.

Cryptic clues are easier than straight clues because they are straight clues with extra information given to make solving them even easier.

3. Hooptedoodle

In this chapter each part of the clue is explained fully.

Synonymcrux

The crux of the clue lies in a synonym, hence the **synonymcrux**. The synonymcrux is always at an end of the clue, either the front end or the rear end, the first word or the last word, or sometimes the first or last group of words. The **synonymcrux** is set in a **bold** typeface in this book.

All other information in the clue is gratuitous, and the entire puzzle can be completed by using the synonymcruxes only. The answer is a synonym for a part of the clue, for example:
~~The lengthy~~ *part* /for\ **a lady** (5) = Helen
Lady = Helen
A lady phoned = Helen phoned

The synonyms may be unusual or rarely used, but are always valid in some specific instance.

Love = zero = 0 = oh = L'oeuf (original French origin of tennis jargon, meaning 'egg') = egg = nil
River = flower (That which flows)
Sewer = seamstress
Griller = interrogator
Weaver = winger = bird = drunk = matmaker

Keyword

The keyword indicates the devices used in the exposition and reveals how the exposition's parts should be manipulated. The devices used reveal the kind of clue. The *keyword* is printed in *italics* in this book.

The keyword explains how to get the answer from the exposition.
~~The~~ len~~gthy~~ *part* /for\ **a lady** (5) = Helen

Helen is *part* of the words '~~t~~he len~~gthy~~'

An entrance /\ I'd *turn in* a̲t̲ (4) = Adit (Adit = Entrance in a mine)
'I'd̲' *turns* back to front, becoming 'di', and is put *in* 'a̲t̲'.

The num is sometimes a keyword. It may indicate a phrase (n,n)
or hyphenated answer (n-n), or it may confirm an anagram when
used in conjunction with another keyword.

There is nothing cryptic about keywords. Keywords mean what
they say. They may be very brief, omitted by ellipsis (eg: 'Heather,
after game' for 'Heather, after playing a game'), or be a bit less than
explicit, but seldom need paraphrasing:

An entrance I'd̲ *turn in* a̲t̲ (4) = Adit
H̲e̲a̲t̲h̲e̲r̲, *after* g̲a̲m̲e̲, **calling the dog** (9) = **Whist**ling

Turn means turn around and in means in. After means after, no
nonsense. Every other word in the clue is altered in some way.
Heather is paraphrased to ling, game to whist, calling the dog to
whistling and an entrance to adit. At is split and I'd reversed, but
the keyword never changes.

However, keywords indicating anagrams are especially varied and
tend to take some form appropriate to the clue or its answer. For
example: *abnormal, affected, agitated, all over, at sea, breaks,
camouflaged, capsizing, chewed, concocted, conversion,
convertible, cooked, cultivated, damaged, drunken, eccentric,
essential, fashion, goes round, idiotic, loosen, manoeuvring,
mince, miraculously, mislaid, mix, mixing, models, moved, must
be dealt with, newly made, odd, opened, order, out, perhaps,
perpetrated, pieces, possibly, problematic, ragged, randomly,
rebelling, rebellious, rebuilt, recipe, redesign, reformed,
remarkable, removed, repair, replanted, rescheduled, resort,*

restoration, resulting in, revised, round, ruptured, shaped, smash, somehow, sort, sorted out, splashed about, squirming, stormy, strangely, switch, terrible, transferred, travelling, tricky, trouble, turmoil, turn, twisted round, uncontrollably, unfortunate, unusual, upset, variation, varieties, weird, worked out, wrecked, wrong, wrongly. All these keywords have been used to indicate anagrams, and the idea is illustrated by the following examples.

Torn skin /of\ *unfortunate* <u>Gl Alan</u> (6) = Agnail
<u>Lie Nora</u> *concocted about* /\ **wing-tip** (7) = Aileron
<u>Rene's</u> *upset* /by\ **expression of contempt** (5) = Sneer
<u>Men test-drive a</u> *convertible* /to get\ **publicity** (13) = Advertisement
<u>Can veto</u> *conversion* /into\ **foreign currency** (7) = Centavo
<u>D~~octo~~r</u> *contains inordinate* <u>greed</u> /making\ **the boat** (7) = Dredger

The more difficult cryptic crosswords have greater latitude in the use of keywords. We see the adventurous setter using 'to eat' as a keyword to mean put inside, thus indicating stacking, which means to set down one bit before another, or between others.

Muddle /as\ <u>Cha~~rle~~s</u> *gets* ~~nothing~~ *to eat* (5) = Chaos
Abbreviate Charles to Chas. Paraphrase nothing to the numeral 0.

The keyword 'medley' is beautifully misleading. Because of its use with 'composed' and 'music' the pasop (the deliberate confusion of Parts Of Speech And Punctuation) succeeds. The synonymcrux must be isolated and seen as an adverb so that it is in grammatical concord with the answer, which is not a past tense verb (as composed would seem to be if the clue had been a sentence, which it is not).

~~Composed~~ /\ <u>a l~~ittle~~ m~~usic~~</u> *medley* (4) = Calm
The answer is a medley of the initial letters of four consecutive words: an acronym (series of initials making a word) requiring abbreviation to one letter. By exception the exposition overlaps the synonymcrux.

Exposition

> For the purpose of instruction, in this book, the <u>exposition</u> is <u>underlined normally when the underlined letters are used in the answer</u>, and <u><u>twice underlined</u></u> where <u>synonyms</u> or <u>multiple devices</u> are required. Unused parts of the exposition are ~~struck through~~ to further contrast the used letters.

Exposition may be defined in several ways:

FIRST DEFINITION
'Exposition: an explanatory statement or account; an explanation or commentary.' (*Oxford English Dictionary*) The exposition explains why only one of the synonyms for the synonymcrux is correct.

SECOND DEFINITION
Expose, reveal, make known.
Thus exposition = revelation or confirmation, e.g., <u>The length</u>y reveals Helen and confirms the correct synonym for **lady**.

THIRD DEFINITION
Ex = out of, or from. Position = place. Thus also out of place, or from its position in the clue or word. For example:

Weekend is K, and the squadron leader is S, the middle of a very short summer is a mm long, Teresa is a confused Teaser and P is the leader of the pack, but a unit is just one piece of ammunition. In the first place, he who dreams happily of bigger income is a dhobi, at least initially. Ask if father has a skiff, since the boat in 'The Heart of Darkness' was Noah's. Smart trams reverse when pupils slip up.

Here is the same paragraph with new fonts:
~~Wee~~k~~end~~ is K, and the <u>squadron</u> *leader* is S, the *middle of* a very short su<u>mm</u>er is a mm long, <u>Teresa</u> is a *confused* <u>Teaser</u> and P is the *leader* of the <u>pack</u>, but a unit is just *one piece of* amm<u>unit</u>ion. *In the first place*, he who <u>d</u>reams <u>h</u>appily <u>of</u> <u>b</u>igger <u>i</u>ncome is a dhobi, at least *initially*. A<u>sk if f</u>ather *has* a skiff, since **the boat** *in*

Exposition (Third definition)

'The Heart of Darkness' was Noah's. Smart trams *reverse* when pupils slip up.

FOURTH DEFINITION

Ex = formerly, or having been. Posit = assume as a fact. Thus, exposit = having been assumed as a fact, and exposition is the act of having so stated on the assumption that the synonymcrux will prove the assumption valid.

Some Dragoons laugh, taking fierce attack (9)

Some ~~Dragoons laugh, taking~~ /\ **fierce attack** (9) = Onslaught

The answer is indeed onslaught, as has been posited in the exposition, and this answer is more easily gleaned from the exposition than from the synonymcrux.

The num is an important part of the exposition. It must not be ignored because it assists in finding anagrams and, where short words are needed, it points to a parabrebit, which is a device by which a word is both paraphrased and abbreviated to a tiny bit of a word:

We /\ *belittle* America (2) = Us
America is paraphrased to United States and abbreviated to US.

Fulcrum

> The fulcrum is the pivotal point on which the two definitions of the answer hinge. It is the point that separates the exposition, with its keyword, from the synonymcrux. It can be the space between words, a punctuation mark, a word or a group of words. It is very useful when recognised because it isolates the synonymcrux for easy identification.

1. The fulcrum is often a word that means that the first definition is a substitute FOR the second:
   The lengthy *part* /FOR\ **a lady** = Helen

2. The first definition IS (the same as) the second:
   The author /IS\ <u>not in</u> = Fielding
3. The first definition BECOMES the second:
   <u>Old lady</u> *caught by* <u>tax</u> /BECOMES\ **a beggar** = vagrant (gran, vat)
4. The first definition MAKES the second:
   Tailless <u>antelope</u> /MAKES\ **dash** = Elan (~~d~~)
5. The first definition is (made) OF the second:
   A prayer /OF\ <u>three short words</u> = Orison (or is on)

Since Don Manley described the fulcrum as a 'link word', some setters have made an effort to include one, and to make it contextually apt. 'Link words' are easy to spot (for example, 'for') and make clues easier by isolating the synonymcrux.

> The fulcrum destroys any semblance the clue may have had to a full sentence by cleaving the clue into two parts that have no influence on each other.

Some ~~forty~~ <u>newts</u> /in\ **the river** (4) = Tyne
<u>Pitch darkness</u> /at\ **twelve** (8) = Midnight
<u>Two</u> *pairs heard* /to be\ **exquisite** (3-3) = Too-too
Spade /in\ ~~second~~ <u>hut</u> (6) = **S**hovel
It is muddy /on the\ ~~second~~ <u>green</u> (5) = **S**lime
<u>Masters sense</u> *trouble* /with\ **second valuation** (12) = Reassessment
Medicine /required for\ <u>child of five</u> in the <u>Orient</u> (7) = Quinine
Half <u>ho~~pe~~</u> <u>no girl</u> /can be found in\ **island capital** (8) = Honolulu
<u>Considered</u> *to be three-quarters* <u>ful~~l~~</u> /when in a\ **reflective mood** (10) = Thought**ful**
Mercenary ∧ <u>to engage the services of</u> <u>Heather</u> (8) = Hire**ling**
Tosses ∧ <u>fish</u> *into a* <u>steamer</u> (6) = **S**ling**s**
<u>I'm</u> *after* ∧ **tax** (6) = Impost
After <u>an</u> <u>alcoholic drink,</u> <u>a</u> ∧ **pain in the chest** (6) = Angina
Letter from Greece ∧ <u>is</u> *sent up with a* <u>note</u> *to* <u>mother</u> (5) = Sigma

See how the fulcrum separates each pair of words to produce a sensible answer:

Lean ∧ <u>over</u> (5) = Spare
Kind ∧ <u>face</u> (4) = Type
Conspicuous ∧ <u>gesture</u> (6) = Signal

Fulcrum

Stay /\ <u>second</u> (7) = Support
General /\ <u>allowance</u> (5) = Grant
Leaves /\ <u>cracks</u> (4) = Goes
Blackish /\ <u>wharf</u>? (5) = Jetty

Here the fulcrum is a comma:

Dance /,\ *taking* <u>drink</u> *after* <u>drink</u> *after* <u>drink</u> (3-3-3) = Cha-cha-cha

Sometimes a dash (or hyphen) is used as a fulcrum, but this happens rarely.

Power /–\ <u>mains at</u> *exchange* (7) = Stamina
Disappearing /–\ but not into thin air (10) = Dissolving
Delicate surgery /–\ <u>yet Dr isn't</u> *involved!* (9) = Dentistry
<u>Child</u> *has* <u>a</u> <u>pound</u> /–\ **the whole amount** (5) = Total
<u>Hat</u> *and* <u>pipe</u> *mislaid* /–\ **in the cemetery?** (7) = Epitaph
<u>Ordinary</u> <u>seaman</u> *first* /–\ **that's odd** (8) = **Ab**normal
<u>Football club</u> ~~lost~~ *twice* /–\ **will go down** (4) = Fall
<u>Spring</u>, *say, on* <u>Elba</u> *possibly* /–\ **how timely** (10) = Seasonable
<u>Work</u> *with* <u>Tim</u>~~ethy~~ *on* <u>one's</u> <u>twitch</u> /–\ **that's hopeful!** (10) =
    Optimistic
Sign indicating <u>where road works usually are</u> /–\ **in front** (5) = Ahead

Num

> The num is the bracketed number of a crossword clue that indicates the number of letters required for each word of the answer, and whether a phrase, compound, hyphen, or single word is required.

Only letters go into the crossword squares. Hyphens, apostrophes (the comma in can't), accents and the spaces between words do not fill a square of their own. They are simply omitted from the grid. For example,
Even this <u>express</u> must come to a <u>halt</u> eventually (3-4,5)
= Non-stop train (12 squares)

Given by Eve, <u>fruit</u> /goes beyond\ **cartilaginous protrusion** (5,5)
  = Adam's apple (10 squares)
Light /,\ <u>charmed object able to grant all one's desires</u> (8,4) =
  Aladdin's lamp (12 squares)
One frequenting /\ a <u>section</u> <u>Hugh</u> *is said to have gone round* (7)
  = Habitué (7 squares)

Originally the num was intended only to save one the trouble of counting the squares of each light when solving clues. Today, the canny cruciverbalist gleans far more information from the num than merely the number of squares in the relevant light. Some puzzles omit the num or limit the information it gives.

Phrases are indicated by putting more than one numeral in the brackets. The numerals are separated by commas. Each numeral indicates a word. The words are always a recognised phrase (n,n).

Succeeding /\ <u>late in life</u> (7,2) = Getting on

Hyphenated words are indicated by the use of a hyphen in place of the comma (n-n).

Volume of regulations a monarch uses? (4-4) = Rule-book

INTERPRETATION OF THE NUM
The num must be read in conjunction with the rest of the clue. When seen in context it reveals much. It is often indicative of devices.

ANAGRAMS
Most anagrams are set in clues as separate words; it is too difficult to find one word that fits the clue. Anagram seekers check every clue to see if any letter groups add up to equal the num:

Things worth remembering /\ <u>I blame Mario</u> *about* (11)
= Memorabilia
The num, name and keyword combine to indicate an anagram.
1+5+5=11

Num (Interpretation of the num)

Things worth = 6+5? No name, nor keyword to support.
Remembering = 11? No name, nor keyword to support.
The num works in conjunction with other information, not alone.

~~Then~~ city's *production* /is\ **artificially produced** (9) = Synthetic
The num, apostrophe and keyword combine to indicate an anagram = 4+5=9

Surgical instrument /\ cut tree *badly*! (7) = Curette
Because 7 = 3+4 only, one is forced to consider an anagram of a surgical instrument. The num isolates the synonymcrux, clearly setting it beyond the fulcrum, which is where the exposition and keyword begin. The trouble is that the clue remains unsolved if one does not know the word 'curette'.

BRIDGEWORDS
The num makes it easier to spot bridgewords (hidden words split by other words). Just search for the required number of letters that bridge the gap between two consecutive words.

~~The len~~gthy *part* /for\ **a lady** (5) = Helen
~~Octo~~ber lingers *in* /\ **the city** (6) = Berlin
Some ~~drag~~ons laugh, ~~taking~~ /\ **fierce attack** (9) = Onslaught

UNDIX
Undixes (or the removal of bits from words) shorten the words they came from, and the num reflects this. For example, East almost always abbreviates to e; without east is thus without e. Ibsen without e is ibsn. Four letters, not five, as in the num of:

Points /made\ *about* Ibs~~e~~n *without* ~~east~~ (4) = Nibs

About indicates an anagram of either made or Ibsen without e. Made is the fulcrum of this clue, leaving ibsn to make nibs from.

CONDIX, PARABREBIT, INITIAL
Reduce this clue to four letters and solve by paraphrasing and abbreviating to less than four letters the word 'prepared', then reduce 'cheer' to its initial and use it as the contents into the container derived from 'prepared'.

~~Prepared~~ *to include* c~~heer~~*leader* /in\ **the body of followers** (4)
= Sect

The setter wants something *to include* something else in four letters? The num helps make the necessary devices obvious since both words in question need reducing.

NUMER, STACKING, CONDIX, PHRASE, PARABREBIT:

<u>One</u> *before* <u>nine</u> *taking in* <u>a</u> <u>novice</u> /who was\ **queuing up** (2,1,4)
= In a line

The numer makes 1 of one. Stacking will put all the right bits in the right order. The condix puts one bit if a word into another bit of a word, al into inine (as concon puts word into word). The phrase occurs in the answer. The parabrebit reduces novice, via learner, to 'l'. One = I, I before nine = inine, inine taking in a novice = inaline because a ~~learner~~ = a L. Thereafter 2,1,4 = In a line. QED. Very hard to do without the num indicating the need for two bitwords (i.e. less than four letters long) and a short word.

PARTWORD
Enormous /\ *part of* the de~~vastation~~ (4) = Vast

Clue number

The clue number is alphanumeric, the alphabetic part indicating whether the answer runs across or down. It must be read in conjunction with the rest of the clue. When seen in context it reveals much. Across and down clues have different indicators of devices (keywords).

HOW CLUE NUMBERS INFLUENCE BACKWORDS

Backwords are reversable words. These keywords acquire special meaning from being in a down clue:

Stake /for\ <u>mountain</u> *climbing* (4) = Ante (backword of Etna)

Saw /\ <u>music</u> *upside down* (5) = Tenon (backword of nonet)

Space /\ <u>to tie *up*</u> (4) = Room (backword of moor)

<u>Have fun</u> *up* /in the\ **bar** (5) = Lever (backword of revel)

Reversals serve as devices in buildwords (i.e. built from bits of clue), and reverse bitwords:

Letter from Greece /\ <u>is</u> *sent up with* <u>a note</u> *to* <u>mother</u> (5) = **Si**gma

<u>It</u> *turns up after* <u>an</u> /\ **opponent** (4) = Anti

Man /\ <u>is</u> *back before* <u>Mon~~day~~</u> (5) = **Si**mon

Or to reverse a partbit:

<u>Ron~~ald~~ *in* c~~ourt~~</u> *bringing up* /\ *tips* /\ **for the waiters** (5) = Tron**c**

Giving out /\ <u>a sound</u> *after* <u>time</u> *is up* (8) = <u>Emit</u>ting

Or to reverse a dix (an odd piece of word):

Portentious /\ <u>doctor</u> *lifted* <u>one</u> *with* <u>common sense</u> (7) = **Om**inous

<u>Daring villain</u> *holds* <u>attorney</u> *up* /in\ **a show of boldness** (7) =
    Bravado

STACKING AND CLUE NUMBERS

When there is no stacking keyword, stacking is assumed to be left to right or top to bottom. The keywords indicating stacking in buildwords are very often dependent on direction.

<u>One</u> *before* <u>nine</u> *taking in* <u>a</u> <u>novice</u> /who\ is **queuing up** (2,1,4)
    = In a line

Region /is\ <u>dry</u> *on top of* <u>the hill</u> (6) = Sector

Hold /\ *tangled* <u>net</u> *over* <u>the river</u> (6) = Tenure

INTERCLUE

Some clues are incomplete on their own and can only be solved with reference to another clue. There is a clear reference to another clue by mention of its number. These clues cannot be solved before those to which they refer. Most often the answer of the first solved must be inserted in place of the referring clue number

11a) **Stay** ∧ **second** (7) = Support
Bible gets 11 across here in church (7) = Lectern
Bible gets SUPPORT here in church (7) = Lectern

18d) **Downfall** /of\ <u>one</u> *in a* <u>hurry</u> (4) = Ruin
Wiping out 18 down (11) = Destruction
<u>Wiping out</u> ∧ RUIN (11) = Destruction

11a) **A record** *some* youngsters ~~cannot endure~~ (4) = NOTE
Change 11, though sound (4) = Tone
Change <u>NOTE</u>, /though\ **sound** (4) = Tone

On rare occasions a word from the first clue must be substituted.
10d) <u>Passage</u> *to* <u>Scottish island</u> ~~learner~~ took was **temporary** (12)
 = Transitional
Startin' badly ∧ *in* 10 down (7) = Transit
<u>Startin'</u> *badly* /in\ **PASSAGE** (7) = Transit

Caveat

Everywhere there is an exception to the rule, and the rules in cryptic crosswords are tenuous and very flexible.

The synonymcrux and the exposition are not necessarily mutually exclusive parts of the clue.

~~Composed~~ a ~~little~~ m~~usic~~ *medley* (4) = Calm

Sometimes there is no synonymcrux, and here the exposition encompasses the entire clue, overlapping the keyword (as it did the synonymcrux in the previous example).
<u>Easily</u> *converse* (6) = Hardly

Synonymtwins have no explicit keywords, and a dubious claim to an exposition. Do they have two distinct synonymcruxes?
Lean ∧ <u>over</u> (5) = Spare

Caveat

There are odd clues that have no synonymcrux, exposition, keyword or fulcrum.

'Man is by nature a political . . .' (Aristotle) (6) = Animal

As a rough guide, based on an analysis of the database on which this book is based:

More than 90 per cent of clues have a synonymcrux, though not necessarily in a single word. It is always at one or the other end of the clue, never hidden in the middle of the clue.

More than 85 per cent of clues have an exposition of some kind.

More than 80 per cent of clues have a keyword. At least 50 per cent of clues have an explicit keyword, and a further 30 per cent have implicit keywords. Implicit keywords are found in the format of synonymtwins (always two words only) and in the num of phrases, as will be seen later. An absence of an explicit keyword can indicate that stacking is assumed left to right or top to bottom.

In <u>archaeological excavation</u> ~~name~~ <u>worker</u> ∧ **showing scorn** (9) = In**dign**ant

About 43 per cent of clues contain a word that acts solely as a fulcrum. A further 7 per cent of clues have a comma or some other punctuation mark that serves as a fulcrum:

<u>Intrude</u> *clumsily* /,\ **lacking experience** (7) = Untried

Another 50 per cent of clues have an implicit fulcrum adjoining the synonymcrux.

Some ~~Drage~~<u>ons laugh , t</u>~~aking~~ ∧ **fierce attack** (9) = Onslaught

Given a different data pool or sample population the figures will be different, but probably not extremely different. The percentages serve only as a rule of thumb.

4. Crossletters

A crossletter is a letter common to two answers. It is a letter in a rech, which is a checked square; one common to two lights. Once one answer has been found the crossletter becomes an important clue for the other answer.

Finding the first answers of a puzzle is always most difficult because of the lack of crossletters. Some grids are more difficult to complete because they are made of four loosely linked subgrids each of which requires its own start.

The grid above shows that if a quarter of the grid is completed only two reches in other quarters contain crossletters; one into each of two quarters. Compare it to the grid on the next page which shows that if the first quarter of the grid is completed four reches in each of two quarters will contain crossletters. Six of these eight crossletters are initial letters. It is obvious that one should try to first complete those clues that give most assistance in the remaining clues when one has a grid with many reches.

Maximising crossletter availability

Try solving clues in numerical order, working with both down and across clues. The crossletters gleaned in this way are more likely to be initials (the first letter of an unsolved answer) than would be if all the across clues were attempted first. By trying all the across clues first one tries them all without any crossletters at all. A mixture of down and across clues in numerical order very quickly yields crossletters.

Try solving those clues first that yield the most initial letters for the next clues. Try solving those clues that have the longest lights, they yield more crossletters than short lights do.

Using crossletters well

All crossletters must be compared to the unsolved clue's letters, especially when a light contains two crossletters. If the answer to an across clue gives x as a crossletter one must check the down clue to see if the clue contains an x.

A match often makes clues such as anagrams, partwords, bridgewords and even buildwords obvious. In this example the crossletter was an x.

<u>Crowd</u> <u>fight</u> /in\ **reporters' room** (5-3) = Press-bo**x**

Searching the down clue for the letter x in the initial place made it childishly easy to solve.

Relating to woody tissue /\ *of some* ~~wa~~<u>x</u>y <u>lic</u>~~hen~~ (5) = **X**ylic

Having the crossletters t and i make the anagram obvious when one checks the clue for the presence of these letters.

Power /–\ <u>mains at</u> *exchange* (7) = Stamina

Crossletters a and h indicate that the same letters in the clue must be closely examined.

<u>The cards</u> *might be* /made\ **stiffer** (8) = Starc**h**ed

Initial crossletters give access to conventional dictionaries and alphabetised crossword lists. If the initial is a consonant the second letter is most likely to be a vowel and vice versa. Consideration of the likelihoods can shorten search time.

Using crossletters well

Internal crossletters are more difficult, but remember to consider the other parts of the clue, spelling rules and common affixes. For example,

Become inactive but get Stan a disguise (8)
a) Stan. The name suggests an anagram
b) Get Stan a. 3 + 4 + 1 = 8. The num confirms the anagram.
c) Disguise the letter order. *Disguise* is the keyword, indicating an anagram.
d) **Become inactive** must be the synonymcrux.
e) The second last letter is t, a crossletter found by solving a previous clue.
f) A consonant is probably flanked by vowels. Very few words end in a, i, o or u.
g) The anagram has only three vowels: a, a, e.
h) The answer probably contains the suffix -ate (maybe ts, nothing else).
i) The suffix -ts would be in concord (grammatically alike in number, tense, gender and part of speech) with becomes, but not with become, therefore the answer cannot end in ts. It must end in -ate.
j) The remaining letters are a, g, n, s, t.
k) Most likely two consonants either side of the vowel.
l) St and ng are common diphthongs. St a ng ate?
m) **Become inactive** = Stagnate.
   Become inactive /but\ get Stan a *disguise* (8) = Stagnate

When stuck for an answer consult a crossword finisher. The finishers list words in order of each letter, with a secondary ordering of another letter. Last letters can be sought in finishing lists and in reverse dictionaries. List surfing can be tedious and soul-destroying. Try it only as a last resort, but remember that it does yield answers. The lists do work and they help to finish puzzles.

5. Concord

Concord is the agreement between words in gender, number, case, person and part of speech. The clue and answer are always in concord, but in their very own special way. The clue is not a sentence, and the whole clue does not have to be in concord with the answer. To understand how concord works in clues the synonymcrux must be separated from the exposition, which must be isolated from the keyword. The separate parts of the clue will be in concord with the answer, or with parts of the answer.

The whole answer will be in concord with the **synonymcrux**.

Parts of the <u>exposition</u> are paraphrased and manipulated but remain in concord with their corresponding parts of the answer. The entire clue is not at all times in concord with the final answer because the clue contains a diversity of parts of speech. For example,

<u>He</u> *has* <u>a</u> <u>fish</u> /for\ **curing** (7) = Healing
He + a + ling = Healing

He = he – Third person singular masculine noun (in clue and answer)
A = a – Indefinite article (in clue and answer)
Fish = Ling – Singular noun, or collective noun (in clue and answer)
Curing = Healing – Present participle (in clue and answer)

Present participles are a joy and a blessing. If the answer is a present participle, then the clue is almost certain to contain one too. Watch out for the -ing suffix.

Pasop

Pasop is a crossword device where p̲arts o̲f s̲peech a̲nd p̲unctuation are deliberately *reversed* or confused in order to mislead.

If a crossword clue is mistaken for a sentence, which it is not, parts of speech and punctuation are often confused. Concord depends on context. The words harry and fiddles can both be used as either noun or verb. (Man's name = Harry = attack often. Violins = fiddles = fidgets.) For example,

Harry can be a fearsome beast with nothing inside him.
Harry /can be\ <u>a fearsome beast</u> *with* ~~nothing~~ *inside him* (7)
    = Drag o on

Harry is not the subject of a sentence; it is the **synonymcrux** of a clue. It stands alone. It is separated from the <u>exposition </u>and *keywords* by the fulcrum. It seems to be a noun, but it is in fact a verb. It is in concord with the answer. The same holds true for fiddles in this extended synonymtwin.

Fiddles made by skilled craftsmen.
<u>Fiddles</u> /made by\ **skilled craftsmen** (7) = Potters

Cryptic clues are in a class of their own, far above the rest, when they resemble a well constructed whole sentence (with its own subject, verb and object). Eg:
Bird /\ *moves out of* <u>danger</u> (6) = Gander.

Concord as an aid

Concord confirms the correct answer. An awareness of concord is invaluable during the attempt to solve.

<u>Tells a</u> *new* /\ **girl** (6)

At a guess either girl or tells will be the synonymcrux. If girl, then the answer will be a noun, singular, feminine, third person. If tells, then the answer is likely to be a verb, present tense. In the latter case the answer probably ends in s, in the former probably not. Tell is also a noun (meaning an artificial mound) in which case one seeks another noun, but plural. What keywords exist? Only three, maybe four.

Tells = homophone
A = Buildword (a with a 5-letter synonym for new girl)
New = Buildword or anagram
(6) = Anagram of tells a, since only 5 + 1 = 6
It's fairly obvious that if the <u>s</u> only is moved to the front of <u>tell a</u> the result is Stella.
<u>Tells a</u> *new* /\ **girl** (6) = Stella. QED.

Part of speech

The grammatical types of words (adjective, adverb, conjunction, interjection, noun, preposition, pronoun, verb) are preserved subject to the separation of the exposition, keyword and synonymcrux. This has been explained.

SINGULAR AND PLURAL
A plural answer always has a plural clue. This is useful with anagrams ending in s.

Sailors /\ *of the* <u>Tsar</u> (4) = Tars

A clue in the singular containing an s is slightly more easily solved because one knows that the s is not a suffix used to form a plural.

Part of speech

PERSON, THE FIRST, SECOND AND THIRD

In this instance the indicators of third persons are loaded because they often point to humers with vocations or jobs and consequently words that end in -er. For example,

He /\ picks things up mechanically (5-6) = Crane-driver

TENSE

The suffixes of verbs indicate tense in all but irregular forms. Take note of the verbal suffixes in the clue, they often recur in the answer.

~~Young~~ *leader* <u>Bill</u> *has* <u>night</u> *out* /\ **sailing** (8) = Yacht**ing**
Rated /\ <u>a page</u> – <u>commended for it</u> (9) = Apprais**ed**
Crooked <u>NCO's</u> /\ **swindles** (4) = Cons

SUFFIXES

All suffixes have a tendency to recur in the answer. Be aware of them, they are an invaluable aid to finding solutions. They tend to isolate the synonymcrux.

<u>Open land</u> *at both ends of* <u>L</u>angley, /\ **generally** (8) = Common**ly**
Notorious /\ <u>gorge I use</u> *by arrangement* (9) = Egreg**ious**

PART TWO

Crossword Devices

1. Devices Used to Construct Answers

Genus and specie

> Genus and specie is a way to find a specific kind of synonym for a word.

Beech and oak are both synonyms of tree. Erica and ling are both types of heather and thus synonymous with heather. The idea is to think of genus and specie metaphorically, and to find specifics in place of generic nouns, just as, for example, girl and boy are generic but Amy and Eric are specific.

Mercenary /\ <u>to engage the services of</u> <u>Heather</u> (8) = Hire**ling**
<u>Heather,</u> *after* a <u>game of cards,</u> /was\ **making a shrill sound** (9)
    = **Whist**ling
Tosses /\ <u>fish</u> *into a* <u>steamer</u> (6) = **Sling**s
<u>Come in</u> *after* <u>fish</u> /and\ **chips** (9) = **Carp**enter
<u>I'm</u> *after* /\ **tax** (6) = Impost
<u>A tax</u> /\ **popular with racegoers!** (5) = Ascot
Council tax /earns\ <u>stern reproof</u> (6) = Rating
<u>Tax</u> *before* <u>1 May</u> /on\ **religious centre** (7) = **Vat**ican
Obliged /to produce\ <u>tax</u> *before* <u>spring</u> (4-5) = **Duty**-bound
Girl /has\ <u>a large</u> <u>drink</u> *as stated* (7) = Abigail
After <u>an</u> <u>alcoholic drink,</u> <u>a</u> /\ **pain in the chest** (6) = Angina
Gave an account /of\ <u>drink</u> *in the* <u>plant</u> (8) = Re**port**ed
Gave a warning /that there\ <u>was no more</u> <u>drink</u> (9) = **Port**ended

1. Devices Used to Construct Answers

Genus and specie

Dance /‚\ *taking* <u>drink</u> *after* <u>drink</u> *after* <u>drink</u> (3-3-3) = Cha-cha-cha
<u>Greek character</u> ~~caught~~ /despite being\ **smart** (4) = **Chi**c
Letter from Greece ∧ <u>is</u> *sent up with a* <u>note</u> *to* <u>mother</u> (5) = Sigma
Holding ∧ *tangled* <u>net</u> *over the* <u>river</u> (6) = Ten**ure**
Film ∧ <u>Caledonian</u> <u>flower</u> (7) = Pict**ure**

Genus and specie synonyms occur in the exposition and in the synonymcrux.

An <u>Irish</u> ∧ **verse?** (8) = Limerick
The scholar /takes\ <u>ages</u> *to* <u>sum</u> *up* (7) = Erasmus
<u>Circle</u> <u>an island</u> ∧ **sultanate** (4) = Oman
<u>Tuneful</u> ∧ **American painter** (8) = Whistler
Vessel ∧ *almost* <u>departed</u> *with the wrong* <u>load</u> (7) = **Gon**dola
Writer /has\ <u>friends</u> *in France* (4) = Amis
Form of transport ∧ <u>that places strain</u> *on* <u>a writer</u> (8) = Rick**shaw**

Macaroni

Macaroni is the importation of a foreign word into English.

Yankee Doodle came to town
A-riding on a pony,
He stuck a feather in his hat
and called it Macaroni.

The song illustrates how macaroni is the affectation of European manners, usually done to impress others. Macaronic verse is a type of verse that originally blended a mixture of Latin and English. The genre later came to include the admixture of any other (especially continental European) language with English. In cryptic crosswords macaroni is the importation of a foreign word into an English word.

In cryptic crossword clues macaroni is commonly used because of the convenience of a new set of bitwords that are gleaned from foreign languages. Macaroni is a delightful way of parabrebitting parts of a clue and a handy solution in the quest for sensible dixes to concatenate (link together like a chain) in buildwords. In *The Penguin Guide to Cryptic Crosswords*, Jack Dunwoody compiles a good list of frequently used macaronic bitwords.

MODERN EUROPEAN LANGUAGES

<u>Who</u> *in France in the* ~~east~~ <u>calling</u> /for\ **the misleading use of doubtful words?** (12) = **Equi**vocation

Ridicule /\ <u>the</u> *French* <u>member</u> *having* ~~nothing~~ <u>on</u> (7) = **La**mpoon

<u>The</u> *French* <u>travel</u> <u>on</u> /\ **the lake** (6) = **la**goon

Alight /\ <u>from</u> *French* <u>coaches</u> (7) = **De**train

Territory /\ <u>of the</u> *French* <u>ch~~urch~~</u> <u>unknown</u> (5) = **Du**chy

<u>Eric</u> *going wild about* <u>the</u> *French* /\ **girl** (6) = **Cl**aire

E~~xiting~~ *start made by* <u>five</u> *in French* <u>street</u> /to produce\ **theatrical work** (5) = **Re**vue

<u>A</u> *French* <u>oil painting</u> ~~perhaps~~ /, *it is*\ **banal** (10) = **Un**original

<u>The</u> *French going in* <u>for</u> /\ **alcoholic liquor** (4) = **Al**es

<u>Wants</u> *to be out of* <u>the</u> *French* /\ **sewers** (7) = **Needle**s

Shock /\ <u>with reference to</u> *German* <u>conjunction</u> (7) = **Astou**nd

Agenda /for\ ed~~ucation~~ *in* *German* <u>school</u> (8) = **Sche**dule

Reprove /\ <u>Scotsman</u> *embraced by* <u>a</u> <u>stunning looker</u> (8) = **Ad**mon**ish**

<u>Day-dreaming</u> *about Spanish* <u>urging</u> /\ **patience** (9) = **Tole**rance

<u>The</u> *Spanish* <u>porter</u> /has\ **to hang on** (4,3) = **Las**t out

LATIN

Latin is treated differently from all other languages since there is no keyword that mentions the language, as in the case of French, German and Spanish.

ANNO DOMINI

<u>Do</u> *include,* <u>these days</u> /,\ **a deep border of wood** (4) = **Dad**o

Macaroni (Latin)

PRO
He has been instructed to vote /\ for two unknowns (5) = **Pro**xy

RE
He lets loose /and is\ about *to* curse *badly* (7) = **Re**scuer
Order /\ quiet about cut (7) = **Pre**pare
Respecting a black *holding* on /, as is\ **quite right** (10) = **Re**asonable
Said again /\ about it *being* a very long time *with* Edward (10)
   = **Re**iterated
Say it again /\ concerning fuel (6) = **Re**peat

MILLE
He's a lot /on\ **edge** (3) = He**m**
Sticky /\ heavy soil *contains* thousands (6) = Clam**m**y

ANTE MERIDIEM
In the morning, corny *sort* /of\ **word formed from initials** (7)
   = **A**crony**m**

DITTO
In *the* same eastern country /,\ **a peninsula consisting of several**
   countries! (9) = In**do**china

ELIZABETH REGINA, EDWARD REX
Judge /gave\ transcript *to* monarch (8) = Recor**d**er

ULTIMO
Mature /\ this time last month (5) = Ad**ult**

OPUS
Opus is Latin for work. Op is its abbreviation, singular, a work.
Magnum opus = Great work. Ops = works, plural.
He *accepted* little work /in\ **expectation** (4) = H**op**e
Object to /\ work *on* model (6) = **Op**pose
Oh dear! /–\ ~~nothing~~ works (4) = **Oop**s
One who is against /\ work *has a* problem (7) = **Op**poser
Weighs down /with\ work *on* printing machinery (9) = **Op**presses

Macaroni (Latin)

ANTE
Rather slow /\ <u>before</u> – <u>and</u> *at the top!* (7) = And**ante**

AD
The man /\ <u>coming to</u> <u>a</u> <u>stop</u> (4) = **Ad**am

VIDE
Type of recorder /on which\ <u>to see</u> ~~nothing~~ ! (5) = **Vide**o

Numer

A numer is a crossword device that exploits verbal associations with numbers, or where graphemes (writing symbols) are both alphabetic and numeric and the ambiguity allows a solution of the clue. Most numers are a parabrebit of which the resultant bitword is addixed to the answer.

ROMAN NUMERALS
I	=	1
V	=	5
X	=	10
L	=	50
C	=	100
B	=	300 (not widely used)
D	=	500
M	=	1000

A horizontal bar placed over a roman numeral multiplies its value by a thousand. The Romans did not know zero; it was not a number to them. 'The idea of placing an I before V to represent 4, or I before X for 9, for example, which makes numbers shorter to write while making them more confusing for arithmetic, was hardly ever used by the Romans themselves and became popular in Europe only after the invention of printing.' (Wells 1987: 60).

Roman numerals use graphemes that are clearly alphabetic. They are very common in cryptic crossword clues. More often than not a number in the clue indicates a Roman numeral in the answer.

Numer (Roman numerals)

ONE
One <u>king</u> <u>is</u> /showing the\ **flag** (4) = Iris
<u>One</u>, *before* <u>nine</u>, *taking in* <u>a</u> <u>novice</u> /who is\ **queuing up** (2,1,4) = In A Line
<u>Tax</u> *before* <u>1</u> <u>May</u> /on\ **religious centre** (7) = Vatican
Small bar /,\ <u>second-class</u> <u>one</u>, *different* <u>sort</u> (6) = Bistro

FOUR
<u>Break</u> *at* <u>quarter</u> *past* <u>four</u> ∧ **feeling fidgety** (7) = Restive
Arranged <u>search</u>, *about* <u>four</u> /, for\ **old records** (8) = Archives

FIVE
~~Exiting~~ *start made by* <u>five</u> *in French* <u>street</u> /to produce\ **theatrical work** (5) = Revue
<u>Five</u> <u>make a mark</u> /on the\ **weed** (5) = **V**etch
Sort out ∧ <u>a</u> *Parisian* <u>quintet</u> *in* <u>real</u> *trouble* (7) = Unravel

SIX
Liberal ∧ <u>whip</u> *goes around* <u>six</u> (6) = Lavish
Countryman ∧ *has* <u>drink</u> *after* <u>6.50</u> (8) = **V**illager
<u>Half a dozen</u> <u>for each</u> ∧ **snake** (5) = **Vi**per
<u>Half a dozen</u> <u>for</u> ∧ **the creeper** (5) = **Vi**per

NINE
Join ∧ <u>a</u> <u>very loud</u> <u>team</u> (5) = Affix
<u>Archdeacon</u> *accepts* <u>nearly ten</u> /from\ **a spiteful woman** (5) = Vixen

TEN
<u>None</u> *over* <u>ten</u> <u>look at</u> ∧ this **flower** (2-3) = Ox-eye

ELEVEN
The hired car ∧ *turned up* <u>at</u> <u>eleven</u> (4) = Taxi

FIFTY
Countryman ∧ *has* <u>drink</u> *after* <u>6.50</u> (8) = Villager
Noisy /and\ <u>love-struck</u> *after* <u>about</u> <u>50</u> (9) = Clamorous

FIFTY-ONE
51 reprimanded /were\ **released** (9) = **Li**berated

NINETY-NINE
Put together 99 ~~tons~~ /for\ **the devotee** (6) = Add**ic**t
The best 99 *forming* /\ the **theme** (5) = Top**ic**
Terrible actors *took* 99 /attempts at\ **the word puzzle (**8) = Acrost**ic**

FIVE HUNDRED
At the wicket *for* 500 /– and\ **got even more!** (9) = Increase**d**

THOUSAND
Puts in /\ a thousand vegetables *perhaps* (8) = **Im**plants
Maintained *about a* thousand /\ **neat** (5) = Ke**m**pt
Sticky /\ heavy soil *contains* thousands (6) = Cla**mm**y

MANY, ETC
Agreeing /with\ many over boy worker (9) = **C**onsonant
He makes deals /with\ many operating farm machinery (10) =
    Contractor
He's a lot on /\ **edge** (3) = **H**e**m**
Actual number /in\ **the kingdom** (5) = Real**m**

ARABIC NUMERALS

ZERO
None *over* ten look at /\ this **flower** (2-3) = **O**x-eye
~~Nothing~~ *found in ruined* castle /except\ **plant used to flavour**
    drink (7) = Alec**o**st
~~Nothing~~ *less than* a lifeless /\ **deity** (5) = W**o**den
Beast /\ *has* ~~nothing~~ *in the* pub (4) = B**o**ar
Harry /can be\ a fearsome beast *with* ~~nothing~~ *inside him* (7) = Drag**oo**n
Type of recorder /on which\ to see ~~nothing~~! (5) = Vide**o**
Blokes encountered ~~nothing~~ *outside that could be* /a\ **souvenir** (7)
    = Ment**o**

Numer (Arabic numerals)

Carthusian *accepting* ~~nothing~~ /but the\ **Last Judgement** (4) = Doom

Cornering /\ top mini saloon? ~~Nothing~~ *in it that is tricky* (14) = Monopolisation

Establish /there is\ ~~nothing~~ *in the* kitty (5) = Found

I throw ~~nothing~~ *up*, /not even these\ **old coins** (5) = Oboli

Oh dear /–\ ~~nothing~~ works (4) = Oops

Opening /\ ~~nothing~~ *pronouncedly* ic~~y~~ *in wild* fire (7) = Orifice

Ridicule /\ the *French* member *having* ~~nothing~~ on (7) = Lampoon

ONE

One king is /showing the\ **flag** (4) = Iris

One, *before* nine, *taking in* a novice /who is\ **queuing up** (2,1,4) = In A Line

Tax *before* 1 May /on\ **religious centre** (7) = Vatican

Small bar /,\ second-class one, *different* sort (6) = Bistro

TEN

Pat~~rick~~ *returns before* ten, *it appears, with* accountant /for\ some **starchy food** (7) = Tapioca

Vigour /of\ bro~~ther~~ *before* ten, ~~it appears~~ (4) = Brio

ELEVEN

Uncommon things /\ *produced by* eleven *in* arrest, ~~perhaps~~ (8) = rarities

ALGEBRAIC NOTATION OF NUMBERS

He has been instructed to vote /\ for two unknowns (5) = Proxy

Territory /\ of the *French* chur~~ch~~ unknown (5) = Duchy

Concise Oxford Dictionary of Current English lists N and n as being '*Math*. an indefinite number' which makes possible:
Indefinite number devour /\ **cattle** (4) = Neat

PARTWORD NUMERS

Partword numbers occur in answers more often than in clues for three reasons.

Numeral graphemes that occur in the clue are transcribed in the answer as alphabetic graphemes (see Roman numerals). Numbers represented by alphabetic graphemes include the words for numbers.

<u>51</u> /and\ **single** (4) = **Lone**

Genus and specie clues have the genus in the clue and the specie in the answer.

<u>Alternative</u> number *first by* /\ **a singer** (5) = **Ten**or
<u>A number</u> <u>assume it to be</u> /\ **fibrous tissue** (6) = **Ten**don
<u>Small number</u> <u>at</u> /\ **Welsh resort** (5) = **Ten**by

Setters compile puzzles by first putting answers in a grid and then devising clues to suit the answers. In this process the clue is broken up into many parts (syllables, partwords, dixemes, affixes and letters). These parts are translated or encrypted into clues. The setter needs to make sense of the parts of the answers to be able to use this method of compilation. Numeric partwords stand out boldly and present a natural course to follow.

<u>Reserve player</u> *gets* <u>no score</u> /– with\ **chilly result** (7) = **Sub**zero
After <u>nine</u>, *there were less than half the* <u>vehicles</u> /in\ **the old capital** (7) = **Nine**veh

Because numeric partwords stand out so boldly they are seldom used in clues. Where they occur in the clue it is solved with ridiculous ease.

Crew /\ *from a* freighter (5) = **Eight**

ANAGRAMS, NOT NUMERS

The presence of a number in the clue does not necessarily indicate a numer. In the anagram the numeric nature of the clue does nothing but mislead.

<u>One real</u> *disaster* /for\ a *girl* (7) = Eleanor
<u>Nine great</u> *varieties of* /\ **fruit** (9) = Tangerine
Another <u>ten clues</u> /\ **one can get one's teeth into** (8) = Esculent
New <u>trains</u>, *about* <u>ten</u> /,\ **staying only a short time** (9) = Transient

NUMER INDICATORS

Vague numbers are indicators of numers, and usually of the genus and specie type. Different puzzles use these words in the same ways but with differing frequencies.

NUMBER

<u>Alternative</u> <u>number</u> *first by* /\ **a singer** (5) = **Ten**or
<u>A number</u> <u>assume it to be</u> /\ **fibrous tissue** (6) = **Ten**don
<u>Small number</u> <u>at</u> /\ **Welsh resort** (5) = **Ten**by
<u>Listen to</u> <u>a number</u> /\ **offer encouragement** (7) = Hear**ten**
Cheered /when\ <u>a number</u> <u>made demands</u> (9) = Ac**claimed**
<u>Large number</u> <u>enquire</u> /about\ the **barrel** (4) = **C**ask
<u>Actual</u> <u>number</u> /in\ **the kingdom** (5) = Realm
'Shake' /–\ <u>a great number</u> *included by* <u>a certain singer</u> (7) = Tremble
Bother /\ <u>any</u> *small* <u>number</u> *inside* (5) = An**noy**
<u>A huge number</u> *retired* /\ **in India** (5) = **A**ssam
<u>Jack</u> *with* <u>a number of lines</u> /\ **will hang around** (5) = Tarry

The function of the word 'Number' changes in the synonymcrux, where it is no longer reduced to a bitword that is addixed to, or into, the answer.

Number one specialist (6) = Egoist
The number one /\ *of the* ~~comm~~unity (5) = Unity
After working out, <u>reveals</u> /\ **a number** (7) = Several
A number /\ <u>had a meal</u>, *we hear* (5) = Eight

MANY

Agreeing /with\ <u>many</u> <u>over</u> <u>boy</u> <u>worker</u> (9) = **C**onsonant
<u>Many</u> <u>hurried</u> *to* <u>be</u> *on the* ~~right~~ <u>lines</u> /with\ the **fruit** (9) = **C**ranberry
<u>Many</u> <u>order</u> <u>suitable</u> /\ **sweet** (6) = **C**omfit
He makes deals /with\ <u>many</u> <u>operating</u> <u>farm machinery</u> (10) =
    Contractor
<u>Many</u> *make* <u>a</u> <u>row</u> /– get\ **abuse** (6) = **M**align
<u>Many</u> <u>arrived</u> *first* /at\ **legendary English town** (7) = Came**lot**
~~A great~~ **many** /\ ~~left~~ <u>to</u> *retire* (3) = Lot

Many, in the synonymcrux, has its conventional meaning.

<u>Go</u> *and* <u>dance</u> *round* /\ the **many-sided figure** (7) = Decagon
Unusual <u>relatives</u> /of\ **many-sided ability** (9) = Versatile
Found out how many /\ *frolicking* <u>deer</u> *were* <u>unable to move</u> *for*
    a start (8) = Numbered

LOT

Lot is used in several ways, but is seldom used to indicate a numer, since it most often retains its other conventional lexical meanings
<u>He</u>'s <u>a lot</u> on /\ **edge** (3) = Hem (Lot = 1000 = m)

These are not numers:
Finished /\ <u>covering the whole lot</u> (3,4) = All over
<u>Flower</u> ~~round~~ <u>a lot of yards</u> /is\ **a tea plant** (8) = Camo**mile**
Force through /\ <u>a lot of nonsense,</u> <u>on the nod</u> (8) = **Bull**doze
<u>Cautioning</u> *about* /\ **knocking the lot down** (10) = Auctioning
<u>Girl</u> <u>able to</u> *recall* /\ **a whole lot of dates** (7) = Almanac

Lot is a bitword, which means that it will appear in answers.

George /gets to\ <u>car-~~parking~~</u> <u>lot</u> *after* <u>one</u> (9) = Autopi**lot**
Randomly <u>fill a lot</u> /of\ the **small fleet** (8) = **Flot**illa
~~A great~~ **many** /\ ~~left~~ <u>to</u> *retire* (3) = **Lot**
<u>Many</u> <u>arrived</u> *first* /at\ **legendary English town** (7) = Came**lot**

IMPLICIT NUMBERS

Implicit numbers are a subset of collective nouns. They are words denoting groups of items of a specific number, volume, length or distance.

0 = love, none, nothing, cipher

Zero is a recent discovery in western mathematics. The great Arab mathematician, Al-Kwarizmi, who in AD 820 wrote the first (modern) mathematical textbook to include zero. Leonardo of Pisa published his *Liber Abaci* in 1202, and in it he described the Indian numbers used by the Arabs, thus introducing zero to the west. Common use of the system in the west was achieved only after the invention of printing. Al-Kwarizmi had found zero in an Indian document. Both the Indians and the Mayans used zero at least 4000 years before the birth of Christ. Did the inhabitants of Atlantis know zero before the Mayans and the Indians?

1   = ace, once, unity, unitary I
2   = deuce, twice, pair, twins, twain, dual, duel, couple, double, bi-, binary, II
3   = trey, thrice, trio, triplets trinity, III
       'In Greek mythology there were three Fates, three Furies, three Graces, three x three Muses, and Paris had to choose between three goddesses. Oaths are traditionally repeated three times. Peter denies Christ three times. The Bellman in *The Hunting of the Snark* says, more prosaically, "What I tell you three times is true!" The world is divided into three parts, the underworld, the earth, and the heavens. The natural world is three dimensional ...' (Wells 1987: 46)
4   = quartet, IV
       Four elements, four humours, four cardinal points of the compass (quarters), four corners of the world, four winds, four rivers of paradise (OT). Einstein's space-time is four dimensional.

1. Devices Used to Construct Answers

4 = Clocks use IIII on normal dials, and IV only if the clock has a Roman strike. Big Ben's dial is incorrect.

5 = quintet, quintuplets, V
Roman numerals increase fivefold or double, alternately – 1, 5, 10, 50, 100, 500, 1000.

6 = half a dozen, sextet, sextuplets

7 = septet, (days in a) week, lucky

8 = crew, octet, (notes in an) octave, octonary, octal

9 = nine numbers, or graphemes, excluding zero, team

10 = decimal, 10 fingers and 10 toes, X

11 = side, the smallest palindromic number and the smallest repunit, a number whose digits are all units. (Wells 1987: 82)

12 = dozen, duodecimal, 12 months, 12 signs of the Zodiac, 12 hours, 12 tone musical scale, 12 inches, 12 old pence. Charlemaine's monetary standard, 1 **L**ibra = 20 **S**olidi = 240 **D**enarii, gave rise to the abbreviation of pounds, shillings and pence as L, s, d. The Romans used only duodecimal fractions: a unit = 12 *Unciae* (whence ounce and inch), an *uncia* = 24 *scrupuli* (whence scruple), one *scrupulus* = 8 *calci*. One *calcus* (whence calculate) was their smallest fraction of a unit.

13 = Unlucky, triskaidekaphobia, 13 cards in a suit, 13 to a baker's dozen. Colin Dexter quotes *Brewer's Dictionary of Phrase and Fable* in *Death Is Now My Neighbour:* **'Thirteen unlucky**: The Turks so dislike the number that the word is almost expunged from their vocabulary. The Italians never use it in making up the numbers of their lotteries. In Paris, no house bears that number.'

14 = a stone (14 lb), a fortnight

15 = team, 15 balls in a snooker triangle

16 = Hexadecimal

20 = a score, vigesimal

24 = 24 hours per day, 24 grains per pennyweight, 24 scruples per ounce

28 = 28 days per lunar month, 28 lb per quarter, 28 dominoes per set

1. Devices Used to Construct Answers

Numer (Implicit numbers)

32   = 32 degrees Fahrenheit at freezing point
37   = 37 degrees Celsius is normal human body temperature
40   = Biblical long time, 40 days in the wilderness, 40 days and 40 nights rain, 40 years wandering in the desert, 40 rods, perches or poles in a furlong (220 yards)
50   = L
52   = 52 weeks per annum (four quarters of 13 weeks), 52 cards in a deck
60   = sexadecimal, as in the Babylonian number system used for mathematical and astronomical work. The Babylonians divided the circle into 360 degrees, each of 60 minutes, each of 60 seconds, and did it a few centuries BC. In consequence we still have an hour (or an angle of one degree) of 60 minutes, each of 60 seconds. These Babylonian measures are the last common measures to resist metrication.
100   = century, 100 degrees centigrade (Celsius) boils water, C
112   = 112 lb per hundredweight
144   = a gross (12 dozen)
153   = 153 fish in Simon Peter's net drawn from the Tiberean sea (NT)
180   = 180 degrees Fahrenheit between freezing and boiling (212–32 = 180), the sum of the angles of a triangle
196   = The palindromic freak: all numbers below 10,000 are palindromes or become palindromic if reversed and added to themselves, repeating the process with each sum. (87,+78=165, +561=726, +627=1353, +3531=4884). 196 does not. Who discovered that? How? Why?
212   = Boiling point of water at sea level in degrees Fahrenheit
500   = D
666   = The number of the Beast in the Book of Revelation
1760 = One mile = 1760 yards = 320 rods, poles or perches = 8 furlongs
2240 = 2240 lb per English ton, one ton = 2240 lb = 160 stone = 80 quarters = 20 hundredweight. In America 2240 lb = one long ton and 2000 lb = a short ton.

Numer (Implicit numbers)

21,000 = The smallest number to use three words in its normal
English description.
635,099 = Vitriolic
With the exception of IV, almost all the information in this list was
gleaned from *The Penguin Dictionary of Curious and Interesting
Numbers*.

PARAPHRASE OF NUMERS
The implicit number is used mutually in the clue and in the answer
and is paraphrased by synonyms.

Going in ~~left~~ *and* ~~right~~ one scoffed ∧ **to wound** (8) = L**acer**ate
Last ∧ but two, to score (10) = Eighteenth
Mark has 100 /of\ **these** (7) = Pfennig
Runs for ∧ **100** ∧ **years** (7) = Century
Second /in\ importance (6) = Moment
Second ∧ of this month (7) = Instant
This issue is one of three ~~to be considered~~ (7) = Triplet
It needs another three, just the same as this, to make a circle (8)
    = Quadrant
About half the clues so described /make\ one angry (6) = Across
Study ~~nothing~~ ∧ **in Ireland** (9) = Co**nn**aught
In *French* ~~nothing~~ /can be\ **put into code** (8) = E**n**cipher
Instrument *comes to* ~~nothing~~ *back* /on\ **glacial ridge** (7) = Drum**lin**
Second eleven ∧ **to collapse** (7) = Sub**side**

The implicit number is often parabrebitted and addixed into the
answer.

Unfriendly ∧ ~~Alfred~~ *goes round* the ducks (5) = Al**oof**
Lucky ∧ *pair of* coppers *in* country dance (5) = Ha**pp**y
Peculiar charm *of a* threesome *endlessly held by* ∧ **an old
    woman of great dignity** (9) = Ma**tri**arch
Medicine /required for\ child of five *in* the Orient (7) = **Quin**ine
Half a dozen for each ∧ **snake** (5) = **Vi**per
Half a dozen for ∧ **the creeper** (5) = **Vi**per
Break *at* quarter *past* four ∧ **feeling fidgety** (7) = Restive
Carol's *after a* single member – ~~nothing~~ ∧ **special** (8) = Imposing
Sort out ∧ a *Parisian* quintet *in* real *trouble* (7) = Unravel

STACKING
When numbers are used as keywords they indicate stacking. Most often the numeral keyword indicating stacking is an ordinal, almost always *first*. Alternatively the numeral is used to indicate the repetition of a dix in the answer.

ORDINALS
Ordinals occur in buildwords, as do most numers. An ordinal indicates the need for stacking unless it is parabrebitted.

Stacking can be indicated by the keyword *'first'*.

Roguish /\ <u>associate</u> , *smashed* <u>cars</u> *first* (8) = **Rasc**ally
<u>American</u> <u>sailors</u> *first* /coming from\ **Paul's birthplace** (6) = **Tars**us
<u>Be</u> *rejecting first* <u>alternative</u> /\ **garment** (4) = **Ro**be
<u>Blend</u> <u>wine</u> *first* /producing\ a **fungicide!** (8,7) = **Burgundy** mixture
<u>City</u> <u>sightseer</u> *first takes* /\ the **cup** (7) = **Eye**bath
Clearly /but\ <u>lazily</u> *having most of the* <u>luck</u> *first* (7) = **Luc**idly
<u>Hard hit</u> <u>trotter</u> *first* /\ **did some marching** (11) = **Foot**slogged
<u>Help</u> ~~rebel~~ *leader first* /in\ **attack** (4) = **R**aid
It is irregular /for\ ~~youth~~ *leader* <u>to make a grab</u> *first* (7) = **Snatch**y
<u>Many</u> <u>arrived</u> *first* /at\ **legendary English town** (7) = **Camel**ot
~~New~~ ~~Testament~~ <u>parable</u> *first* /about\ **old money** (6) = **Tale**nt
<u>Novice</u> <u>led</u> *astray first* /at\ **a small wooded hollow** (4) = **Del**l
<u>Ordinary</u> <u>seaman</u> *first* /–\ **that's odd** (8) = **Ab**normal
Prudent /\ <u>girl</u> *removed* <u>fur</u> *first* (6) = **fru**gal
<u>Ray</u> <u>angry</u> *first* /with\ **light coming from the side** (9) = **Cross**beam
Remained /\ <u>unmoved</u> <u>yet rose to one's feet</u> *first* (5,5) = **Stood** still
Salute /\ <u>the members</u> <u>who are here</u> *first* (7,4) = **Present** arms
Scientist from the <u>country</u> *first* /\ **a student of antiquities** (12) =
    Egyptologist
<u>See</u> *differently first* <u>signal</u> /in\ **jargon** (12) = **Telegraph**ese
Tries /\ <u>at</u> *first* and <u>allures</u> (8) = **At**tempts
<u>Watched</u> <u>overchest</u> *first* /that was\ **protected** (11) = **Safe**guarded
Without initiative /, but\ <u>I ~~have~~</u> <u>to succeed</u> *first* (7) = **Pass**ive
Brown /\ <u>pies</u> *cooked first of* <u>a~~ll~~</u> (5) = Sepia

When an ordinal is not indicative of stacking it is usually parabrebitted. The jargon of these parabrebits is well worth remembering because it is characteristic of cryptic crossword clues.

Went first *round the* snake /and\ **climbed up** (8) = Lad**dered**
Czech, say, went first /and\ **governed** (10) = Contro**lled**
Twin /\ went first *with* a word of hesitation *by* the river (10) = Tweed**ledum**
Went first *round* ancient city /\ **one had been attracted to** (5) = Lur**ed**
Graduates before long *with* first /\ **instrumentalist** (10) = Bassoon**ist**
Living /\ was first in *French* church (9) = Existence (Ex **ist** en CE)
Aegean islands /are\ first class – no one *returns* (5) = Ion**ia**
Second eleven /to\ **collapse** (7) = Sub**side**
Again allow /\ **to offer for rent a second time** (5) = Re**let**
It is muddy /on the\ ~~second~~ green (5) = S**lime**
Small bar /,\ second-class one, *different* sort (6) = B**istro**
Spade /in\ ~~second~~ hut (6) = S**hovel**
Cheat /–\ twice, *almost* (3-4) = **Two**-time
Said *before second half of* ~~July~~ /\ **in the appointed manner** (8) = Stated**ly**
Pur**est** *(not* fifth-rate*) sort* /of\ **oil** (5) = Turps
Stop /\ record on *other* unit, fifth rate (11) = Discontinu**e**

By exception, ordinals occur in the synonymcrux where they have their conventional meaning.

Possibly first /\ service book (7) = Ordinal
First post /\ lady? (5) = Penny
Masters sense *trouble* /with\ **second valuation** (12) = **Re**assessment
Second /in\ importance (6) = Moment
Second /\ of this month (7) = Instant
Stay /\ second (7) = Support
~~Henry~~ prepared *to go in front of* /\ **the third son** (4) = Seth
The **fourth** /\ part (7) = Quarter

Numer

UNDIX IN NUMERS
When the numeral is used to indicate the use of a dix in the answer there is usually another keyword that blatantly indicates stacking. The need for stacking is obvious even without the second keyword since its use is implicit in the undix. The indicated dix is found in the clue and repeated in the answer.

Half <u>ho~~pe~~ no girl</u> /can be found in\ **island capital** (8) = **Ho**nolulu
<u>Said</u> *before second half of* ~~July~~ /\ **in the appointed manner** (8)
   = Stated**ly**
After <u>half-time,</u> I ~~have~~ the <u>right</u> /\ **fur** (7) = **Min**iver
<u>Considered</u> *to be three-quarters* <u>fu~~ll~~</u> *when in a* /\ **reflective mood** (10)
   = Thought**ful**

Occasionally the numeral indicates that the repetition of the dix is itself repeated.

<u>Val~~erie~~</u> *is protected by two* <u>accountants</u> <u>from</u> *French* /\ **parade** (9)
   = **Ca**val**ca**de
Lucky /\ *pair of* <u>coppers</u> *in* <u>country dance</u> (5) = Ha**pp**y
<u>But not</u> *during* <u>the night,</u> *two* ~~levers~~ *initially* /\ **loiter** (5) = Da**ll**y

ODD NUMERS
Odd numers often rely on the phenomenon that numeric words and phrases have acquired specific meanings devoid of numeric meaning.

Does it come at the end of the /\ **eleventh hour?** (4,6) = Last minute
<u>Don't fill up so often</u> /\ **for nothing** (10) = Chargeless
Territory where bartering costs nothing? (4,5,4) = Free trade area
Six hours /\ for settling accounts? (7-3) = Quarter-day
One having nine tenths of the law (9) = Possessor
<u>Pitch darkness</u> /at\ **twelve** (8) = Midnight

Non-numeric words, on the other hand, have also acquired a sense of numeric meaning. In these examples the numeric meanings (of the answers) are ammeled into the clue.

Absolutely nothing, only bacon and eggs? (3,1,7) = Not a sausage
Did nothing original (8) = Imitated
Half a mo' (5,6) = Split second
<u>Pitch darkness</u> /at\ **twelve** (8) = Midnight
Territory where bartering costs nothing? (4,5,4) = Free trade area
Halfwit /\ <u>finds it easy</u> ~~to put~~ <u>weight</u> **on** (9) = Simpleton
<u>A birdie or one better</u> *in the* <u>valleys</u> /of\ **course** (10) = Glen**eagle**s
<u>Like</u> <u>measures</u> /of\ **quarter sessions** (7) = Assizes

TRADITIONAL GROUPS
One in seven /\ *is from* ~~men vy~~<u>ing for top jobs</u> (4) = Envy (Seven
   deadly sins)
Reflect on /\ <u>one of a group of nine</u> (4) = Muse (Nine muses of
   Greek mythology)

Odd numeric references may include splitwords, homophones,
puns, dates, bridgewords and buildwords.

It measures /\ <u>two attributes of a gymnast</u> (6,7) = Spring balance
<u>Alastair</u> *in three words* /produces\ **a final work** (4-4) = Swan-
   song (A last air)
<u>Two</u> *pairs heard* /to be\ **exquisite** (3-3) = Too-too
A number /\ <u>had a meal</u>, *we hear* (5) = Eight
<u>Two sides converge on this</u> /\ **kick** (6) = Corner
Figure /\ of eight (7) = Octagon
15th /\ ~~saint~~ <u>inside</u>! (7) = Swithin (St Swithin's day = 15th)
Highlight /of\ '**70s fashion trousers**? (5) = Flare
Some ~~forty new~~<u>ts</u> /in\ **the river** (4) = Tyne
Sort out /\ <u>a</u> *Parisian* <u>quintet</u> *in* <u>real</u> *trouble* (7) = **Un**ravel

2. Devices Used to Deconstruct Clues

Pasop

> The word pasop is a reverse acronym of '**p**arts **o**f **s**peech **a**nd **p**unctuation' which are put out of order in order to misdirect.

The best synonymtwins use this device. They each appear to be a noun and its descriptive adjective, but must be read as two nouns in order to solve the clue.

Word ∧ <u>case</u> (11) = Portmanteau
Festival ∧ <u>season</u> (7) = Harvest
Brush ∧ <u>plant</u> (5) = Broom
Round ∧ <u>letter</u> (8) = Circular
Quite ∧ <u>guiltless</u> (5) = Clean (quite = completely = clean)
Rich ∧ <u>wit</u> (5) = Comic
Statutory ∧ <u>walk</u> (14) = Constitutional
Drill ∧ <u>practice</u> (8) = Exercise
Alloy ∧ <u>fuse</u> (5) = Blend
African ∧ <u>wasteland</u> (4) = Moor

Any parts of speech may be confused. Here are some verbs that are confused with nouns andor adjectives.

Spring /an\ <u>expression of surprise</u> (4) = Well
Assemble ∧ <u>fitting</u> (4) = Meet
Stay ∧ <u>second</u> (7) = Support
Staunch ∧ <u>supporter of a flower</u> (4) = Stem
Press men /in\ <u>China town</u> (8) = Shanghai
Mis-hit ∧ <u>a boundary</u> (4) = Edge
Do not leave ∧ <u>shore</u> (4) = Stay
Fiddles /made by\ <u>skilled craftsmen</u> (7) = Potters

<u>Neat</u> ∧ **barrier** / \ **on the way** (6-4) = Cattle-grid (Neat must be paraphrased as a noun. It is not an adjective.)
Dreamers /who are\ <u>thought</u> <u>heels</u> (9) = **Ideal**ists (Thought is a noun, not a verb. Heels is a verb, not a plural noun.)
The **fourth** ∧ <u>part</u> (7) = Quarter (A rare extended synonymtwin that uses a definite article instead of the indefinite article in order to misdirect. The result is that fourth is read as an ordinal adjective instead of as a fractional adjective or a noun.)

Phrases sometimes need to be broken up and divided between the synonymcrux and the exposition so that the conjunction becomes the fulcrum.

Country /and\ <s>western</s> <u>tipple</u> (5) = Wales

Punctuation marks are most likely to function as the fulcrum of the clue but sometimes the pasop will ignore punctuation and separate the parts of the clue in the middle of a phrase.

Last ∧ <u>but two, to score</u> (10) = **E**ighteenth
Spread ∧ <u>ruin</u> – <u>got</u> *about* <u>a</u> <u>pound</u> (9) = Marmalade
Being <u>gross, a heel</u> ∧ **will take whatever comes** (8) = Fatalist

The separation of ideas does not occur at the comma, but after heel in the middle of a coherent phrase.

Setting out, <u>steer</u> <u>ship</u> *inside* ∧ **locks** (7) = Tresses (Set out the letters of steer, and insert ship. The punctuation misleads.)

In the odd instance a capital letter can be used to mislead.

Left behind ∧ <u>by Will</u> <s>perhaps</s> (10) = Bequeathed

Stacking

> Stacking refers to the concatenation of dixes when building a word.
>
> The metaphor is derived from the way in which children use wooden blocks with letters on them to build words. In crosswords the dixes may be stacked in any order (up, down, backwards, forwards, in between, around), depending on the instruction contained in the keywords. In the absence of any instruction, stacking is from left to right or from top to bottom.

A city /\ <u>club</u> *with* <u>aspiration</u> (4) = Ba**th**
Girl /has\ <u>a</u> <u>large</u> <u>drink</u> *as stated* (7) = A**big**ail
<u>Bird</u> *to* <u>irritate</u> ~~right~~ /\ **beetle** (10) = Cock**chafer**
<u>A</u> <u>male</u> /\ **go-between** (5) = A**gent**
<u>Hinder</u> <u>a few</u> /being\ **unwieldy** (10) = Cumber**some**
Sooner /have\ <u>nobleman</u> <u>that is</u> ~~right~~ (7) = Ear**lier**
<u>Stop</u> <u>acting</u> /\ **when the game is finishing** (7) = **End**play
<u>Worker</u> <u>to complain bitterly</u> /about\ **the banister** (8) = Hand**rail**
<u>Principal</u> <u>route</u> /for\ **progress** (7) = Head**way**
Alight /\ <u>from</u> *French* <u>coaches</u> (7) = **De**train
Ward off /\ <u>Catherine</u> *before end of* ~~day~~ (5) = **Parr**y
From ~~north-east,~~ ~~Augustus~~ /brought\ **hot wine** (5) = Negus

Even when letter order is reversed or anagrammed the order of stacking of dixes remains unchanged.

Antique type /,\ <u>for example</u> – <u>painty</u> *sort* (8) = **Eg**yptian
<u>Everyone</u> *needs* <u>a nice</u> *exciting* /\ **marriage** (8) = **All**iance
~~Right~~ *up to* <u>deny</u> *alterations* /that are\ **with it** (6) = **Tr**endy

However, the order of stacking is sometimes far from simple. It may be reversed.

Salute /the\ <u>members</u> <u>who are here</u> *first* (7,4) = Present arms
<u>Scientist</u> *from the* <u>country</u> *first* /\ **a student of antiquities** (12)
   = Egypt**ologist**

<u>Be</u> *rejecting first* <u>alternative</u> ∧ **garment** (4) = Ro**be**
<u>Owner</u> *distracted after* <u>vehicle</u> /gets\ **crushed** (8) = **Car**eworn
Bent /on\ <u>bet</u> *after a* <u>bright idea</u> (9) = Hunchback

One dix may be stacked inside another. The keywords instruct that one word be put into another or that one word be put around or about another.

Agenda /for\ <u>e~~ducation~~</u> *in* <u>German school</u> (8) = Sched**ule**
Bore /is\ *shockingly* <u>rude</u> *in the* <u>end</u> (7) = En**dure**d
<u>Otto</u> <u>hurried</u> *into* ∧ **port in Italy** (7) = O**tran**to
<u>Thus,</u> *about* <u>record time</u> /, found\ **it was poisoned** (6) = Se**p**tic
<u>Go</u> *back into* <u>Linden's</u> ∧ **city** (7) = Lim**oge**s
Muddle /as\ <u>Cha~~rles~~</u> *gets* ~~nothing~~ *to eat* (5) = Cha**os**
Enormous ∧ <u>deficit</u> *in* <u>solid fuel</u> (8) = Colos**sal**

One part of the clue may be required to be put into another part of the clue.

<u>Who</u> *in France in the* <u>ea~~st~~</u> <u>calling</u> /for\ **the misleading use of doubtful words?** (12) = Equivocation
<u>Lie</u> *about* <u>exercise</u> *and* <u>about</u> ∧ **regard for it** (7) = Res**pect**
   (This must be read as: <u>Rest</u> *about* <u>P~~hysical~~</u> <u>E~~xercise~~</u> *and* <u>C~~irca~~</u>
   regard for it)
Going in <u>le~~ft~~</u> *and* <u>ri~~ght~~</u> <u>one</u> <u>scoffed</u> ∧ **to wound** (8) = La**cera**te

3. Devices Used to Reconstruct Clues into Answers

Abbreviation

Abbreviation is one of the most important and most common devices in cryptic crosswords. Apart from everyday common abbreviations, which abound in crosswords, there are several other methods of abbreviation that are used in cryptic crosswords. They are: initial letter, capital letters, apostrophe of elision, crossword jargon, parabrebit, parabreve, numers and elements.

INITIAL LETTER

> A vast number of words are normally abbreviated to their initial letter. Besides these, the cryptic crossword will abbreviate many other words to initials, too. These initial letters are used in crosswords to build answers. Initials are an easy way to undix a letter from a word and use it in building the answer. Initials feature prominently in transinsertions and buildwords.

DISHEARTENMENT
Goldfinch *dropped* dead /?\ **Restate main points!** (5) = Recap
(Redcap = Goldfinch)
Element /\ Walter left *out* (5) = Water

TRANSINSERTIONS
A great **many** /\ left to *retire* (3) = Lot
A mountain dweller /\ *found another* road ran north (8) = Andorran
Cult *took* early *lead in the wearing* /of\ **armour** (5) = Culet
Denis *could be* right /, it's\ **more derogatory** (6) = Snider
Harem slave found /\ squalid *mess, and* opposite *extremes* (9)
    = Odalisque
Innocent /\ Bess *about to prepare* meal *on* lake (9) = Blameless
It's a puzzle /having\ *comic* actors in charge (8) = Acrostic

Abbreviation (Initial letter)

Maker of laws ∧ some *break on* ~~Sunday?~~ (5) = Moses
New cars ~~parking~~ /on\ **steep slope** (5) = Scarp
New rector *accepts* ~~fellow~~ /,\ **a small farmer** (7) = Crofter
Offender ∧ cut lip *badly* ~~right~~ *inside* (7) = Culprit
Old boat /from\ Arno has *surprisingly* ~~keeled~~ *to start with* (5,3)
   = Noah's Ark
Quickly ∧ on top *struggling to contain* ~~rebel~~ *leader* (6) = Pronto
~~Red~~*head in with unusually* stout ∧ **instructors** (6) = Tutors
Somehow get Eve to a ~~river~~ ∧ **gorge** (7) = Overeat

BUILDWORDS
~~Caught~~ *by* one with an inclination /*to become*\ **a char** (7) = Cleaner
Vessel I ~~caught~~ /in\ **terror** (5) = Panic
~~Cold?~~ Warming up /in\ **fleecing** (8) = Cheating
Writing *up about* ~~cold~~ man's ∧ **separation** (6) = Schism
~~Composed~~ a ~~little~~ ~~music~~ *medley* (4) = Calm
~~Conservative~~ girl ~~in-charge~~ /,\ **a model** (7) = Classic
Join ∧ ~~conservative~~ on border (8) = Converge
Covered ∧ in skilful ~~depth~~ (7) = Insured
~~Daughter~~ – one /of\ **23** (4) = Done
   (Even without the benefit of the referent interclue one can see
   how daughter is abbreviated to d and added to one.)
Port /that is\ a ~~credit~~ *to the* ~~east~~ (4) = Acre
Antelopes /from\ ~~eastern~~ countries (6) = Elands
Major ~~eastern~~ ∧ **state of USA** (5) = Maine
Catch a glimpse of ∧ ~~English~~ mole, ~~perhaps~~ (4) = Espy
Catch sight of an ∧ ~~English~~ agent (4) = Espy
~~Fellow~~ *with* no drink /in the\ **market-place** (5) = Forum
Settled *after* a ~~fellow~~ ∧ **joined** (7) = Affixed
Spots ∧ one ~~general-manager~~ *taking* a model *into the* ~~station~~ (8)
   = Stigmata
~~Henry~~ and I excel /, *despite*\ **disadvantage** (8) = Handicap
~~Henry~~ prepared *to go in front of* ∧ **the third son** (4) = Seth
Last year's winner /is in\ ~~hospital,~~ not so young (6) = Holder
Grotesque ∧ worker ~~in-charge~~ (5) = Antic
Solid ∧ young scout ~~in-charge~~ (5) = Cubic
Consider how /to\ spare *the* ~~king~~ (5) = Think

3. Devices Used to Reconstruct Clues into Answers

Abbreviation (Initial letter)

Marsupial /to\ ~~knock-out~~ the <u>boy</u> *almost* (5) = **Ko**ala
<u>Passage</u> *to* <u>Scottish island</u> ~~learner~~ *took* /was\ **temporary** (12)
   = Transitiona**l**
Attack ∧ <u>animal, one</u> **l** ~~left~~ (6) = Assai**l**
Become depressed /when\ ~~left~~ <u>suffering</u> (8) = Languis**h**
Coal ∧ ~~left~~ *on* <u>fire</u> (7) = **L**ignite
<u>Drink</u> ~~left~~ /for\ **a bird** (4) = Tea**l**
<u>Equipment</u> *returned and* ~~left~~ /with\ **the young lady** (4) = Gir**l**
Figure-skating jump ∧ <u>cut</u> *on* the <u>left</u> (4) = **A**xe**l**
Going in ~~left~~ *and* <u>ri~~ght~~</u> <u>one</u> <u>scoffed</u> ∧ **to wound** (8) = **L**acerate
<u>L~~eft~~ part of church</u> ∧ **to fall into disuse** (5) = **L**apse
<u>Record</u> ~~left,~~ *another* <u>hit</u> ∧ **made of stone!** (8) = Monolit**h**
<u>Remains</u> *with* <u>one</u> **l** ~~left~~ ∧ **found on the boat** (8) = Staysai**l**
Small stones ∧ ~~left~~ *under* <u>the tomb</u> (6) = Grave**l**
Trees ∧ *making* ~~long~~<u>bows</u> (7) = **L**arches
Amusing /yet\ <u>firm</u> <u>m~~ale in charge~~</u> (5) = Comi**c**
<u>In archaelogical excavation</u>, ~~name~~ <u>worker</u> ∧ **showing scorn** (9)
   = Indignan**t**
<u>N~~ame~~</u> *on* <u>chest</u> /of\ **police spy** (4) = **N**ark
<u>Plead</u> *for* <u>n~~ame~~</u> /of\ **coward** (6) = Crave**n**
<u>Change</u> <u>n~~ew~~</u> <u>rota,</u> *change* ∧ **current generator** (10) = Alternato**r**
From <u>n~~orth-east,~~</u> <u>Augus~~tus~~</u> /brought\ **hot wine** (5) = **N**egus
<u>Ol~~d-boy~~</u> *has* <u>desire</u> /to be\ **not quite square** (6) = **Ob**long
One *follows* ∧ <u>smash-hit</u> *with* <u>operational r~~esearch~~</u> (9) = Successo**r**
<u>A p~~age~~</u> <u>sounding</u> ∧ **charming** (9) = **A**ppealing
George /gets to\ <u>car-~~parking~~</u> *lot* *after* <u>one</u> (9) = Autopilo**t**
Temple /of\ <u>deity</u> *ringed by* ~~parking~~ <u>motorists</u> (6) = **P**agoda
Minute portion /of a\ <u>p~~enny~~</u> <u>item</u> (8) = Particl**e**
<u>P~~enny~~</u> <u>bound</u> /to be\ **supple** (7) = **P**liable
<u>P~~enny~~</u> *had less than* <u>one</u> <u>quarrel</u> /with the\ **high priest** (7) = **P**ontiff
<u>P~~resident,~~</u> <u>transported</u> *all around* /, is\ **exhausted** (5) = Spen**t**
Petition /for\ <u>p~~roportional representation~~</u> <u>always</u> <u>ri~~ght~~</u> (6) = **P**rayer
<u>P~~ublic relations~~</u> <u>unity</u> /may reveal\ **bias** (9) = **P**roneness
<u>Q~~uestion~~</u> *a* <u>sailor</u> *about* ∧ **a Gulf country** (5) = **Q**atar
Foreman ∧ <u>to ignore</u> <u>Re~~x~~</u> (8) = Overseer (Setting error: overlook?)
<u>Restrain</u> <u>Re~~x~~</u> /from\ **making a row** (4) = Tie**r**
<u>Author</u> *on the* <u>ri~~ght~~</u> ∧ **fence** (7) = Barrie**r**

Balcony ∧ ~~right~~ *inside the* <u>cooking area</u> (7) = Gallery
<u>Father</u> ~~right~~ *to accept* /and\ **participate** (7) = Partake
Filled with tension ∧ ~~right~~ *in the said* <u>stronghold</u> (7) = Fraught
Fireside ∧ ~~right~~ *in the* <u>waste land</u> (6) = Hearth
<u>Fit</u> ~~right~~ *into* ∧ **quarrel** (5) = Argue
<u>It falls</u> ∧ ~~right~~ *into* <u>sink</u> (4) = Drip
Jog ∧ ~~right~~ <u>round</u> *in* <u>race</u> (4) = Trot
<u>Many</u> <u>hurried</u> *to* <u>be</u> *on the* ~~right~~ <u>lines</u> /with\ **the fruit** (9) = Cranberry
~~Right~~ *back to* <u>deny</u> *alterations* /that are\ **with it** (6) = Trendy
~~Right~~ *in* <u>place</u> ⌐*leave* /a\ **positive electron** (8) = Positron
~~Right~~ <u>rower</u> /gives a\ **loud cry** (4) = Roar
A doctor ∧ <u>sees</u> a ~~rotter~~ *with some* <u>hesitation</u> (5) = Curer
Man ∧ *makes* <u>appeal</u> *to* <u>energetic</u> ~~royal~~ (6) = Oliver
~~Rugby,~~ *over* <u>an hour</u> ∧ **in Germany** (4) = Ruhr
15th /finds\ ~~saint~~ *inside!* (7) = Swithin
It is muddy ∧ *on the* ~~second~~ <u>green</u> (5) = Slime
Spade /in\ ~~second~~ <u>hut</u> (6) = Shovel
<u>Well</u> ~~sergeant-major~~ /is\ **fit** (5) = Spasm
<u>Did</u> *go round* ~~southern~~ <u>gatehouse</u> /,\ **having been evicted** (9) = Dislodged
<u>Gibraltar</u> *that is* ~~south~~ /of\ **the mountains** (3,7) = The Rockies
Sycophants ∧ ~~succeeded~~ *in* <u>Arabian republic</u> (3-3) = Yes-men
It is used for dressing wounds /if\ ~~left in time~~ (4) = Lint
<u>Put together</u> <u>99</u> ~~tons~~ /for\ **the devotee** (6) = Addict
Admits ∧ <u>US troops</u> *brought about* ~~victory in Europe~~ (5) = Gives
Country /and\ ~~western~~ <u>tipple</u> (5) = Wales

INITIALS INDICATED BY KEYWORDS

THE KEYWORD 'BEGINNING OF'
Beginning of ~~thirties~~ <u>turbulent</u> ∧ **depression** (6) = Trough

THE KEYWORD 'HEAD'
~~Chapter~~ *head* <u>remains</u> /with\ **the money** (4) = Cash
Chatty ∧ <u>lecture</u> *at* <u>teatime</u> *perhaps by* ~~egg~~*head* (9) = Talkative
Deputise /for\ ~~new deputy~~*-head in* <u>disgrace</u> (5,2) = Stand in
In the <u>country</u> *head of* ~~house~~ ∧ *is* **right to vote** (9) = Franchise

Abbreviation (Initials indicated by keywords)

Sensual /\ ~~red~~*head in the* <u>waterway</u> (6) = Carnal
~~Skin~~ *head* <u>drove off</u> /on\ **a lively horse** (5) = Steed

THE KEYWORD 'INITIALLY'
<u>Adolescent</u> ~~youth~~ *initially* /makes\ **very little** (5) = Teeny
<u>But not during the night,</u> *two* ~~lovers~~ *initially* /\ **loiter** (5) = Dally
Shed /that's\ ~~no-good~~ *initially in* <u>Scotch mist</u> (6) = Hangar

THE KEYWORD 'LEADER'
<u>Do not stand</u> a ~~revolutionary~~ *leader* /taking\ the **instrument** (5) = Sitar
Gracious /\ ~~group~~ *leader is in the* <u>country</u> (6) = Benign
<u>Help</u> ~~rebel~~ *leader first* /in\ **attack** (4) = Raid
<u>Hurried</u> *with* ~~Dutch~~ *leader's* /\ **currency** (4) = Rand
It is irregular /for\ ~~youth~~ *leader* <u>to make a grab</u> *first* (7) = Snatchy
Leading ~~entertainer~~ *gets in* <u>quick</u> /\ **banquet** (5) = Feast
Leading ~~seaman,~~ *given* <u>short notice</u> /, was\ **unhappy** (3) = Sad
<u>Left</u> *with* ~~revolutionary~~ *leader* /,\ **he is past recovery** (5) = Goner
<u>Prepared</u> *to include* ~~cheer~~*leader* /in\ the **body of the followers** (4)
    = Sect
To <u>every one</u> *the* ~~youth-~~*leader* /is\ **a friend** (4) = Ally

THE KEYWORD 'SMALL'
Careless /with\ <u>smack,</u> *small* ~~dose~~ <u>has</u> *destroyed* (8) = Slapdash

THE KEYWORD 'START'
Attacked /\ <u>this balloon</u> *at start of* <u>~~day~~</u> (8) = Barraged
Start to ~~speak~~-<u>out</u> /as\ **an orator?** (5) = Spout
Vulture /\ <u>to join</u> *in* <u>early</u> *perhaps, about start of* <u>~~morning~~</u>? (11)
    = Lammergeyer

CAPITAL LETTERS

Capital letters in a clue are sometimes an indication that the capital letters are to be addixed in building the answer.

Cherished ~~Commanding Officer~~ *inside* /\ **showing early development** (10) = Pre**co**cious

Puzzle /\ for legal scholar *up from* ~~Middle East~~ (7) = Prob**le**m
(A down clue, reversing ME after pro Bachelor of Law)

Figures /of\ *little* ~~house~~ *with* doctor *in* ~~Rhode Island~~ (6) = **R**hombi

~~New Testament~~ parable *first* /about\ **old money** (6) = Ta**le**nt

State 'I love ~~Western Australia~~' (4) = Io**wa**

~~Special Constable~~ criticised /and\ **discarded** (8) = **S**crapped

Soldier hurried *with* you *in France to* ~~Los Angeles~~ /on seeing\ **a hairy horror** (9) = Tarant**ula**

River /\ ~~Severn~~ *starts in the* ~~United Kingdom~~ (3) = **Usk**

Humble /\ cleric *going round* ~~Middle East~~ (6) = Deme**an**

Satisfy /\ ~~Poet Laureate~~ with no difficulty (6) = **Pl**ease

Egg *in* ~~Papua New Guinea~~ /producing\ **a foul smell** (4) = **P**ong

Dismantle /a\ ~~United Nations~~ oil installation? (5) = **Un**rig

Part /of\ the ~~New Testament~~ *initially revised* (5) = Ten**th**

Piece of music /\ one *found in the* ~~New Testament~~ (5) = **N**onet

Maker of laws /\ some *break on* ~~Sunday?~~ (5) = Mose**s**

Ambassador /\ *presents* award *to* ~~Tory~~ *leader* (8) = Diploma**t**

Living luxuriously /\ in the ~~Cape~~ *with* one's paramour (2,6) = In **c**lover

It's *about* a ~~Latin~~ fellow's /\ **charm** (8) = **T**alisman

Gary ~~North~~ *upset* /\ **showing extreme displeasure** (5) = Angry

Crooked NCO's /\ **swindles** (4) = **Con**s

Small hotel /\ in *the* ~~Norwegian~~ *capital* (3) = I**nn**

Bill *goes to the* ~~North~~ /\ **gate** (7) = Poster**n**

~~Old~~ PC ~~North~~ /is\ **a character** (7) = **O**micron (PC = personal computer = micro)

Open land *at both ends of* ~~Langley~~ /,\ **generally** (8) = Common**ly**

One frequenting /\ a section Hugh *is said to have gone round* (7) = **H**abitué

Abbreviation (Capital letters)

Capitals may also indicate that a group of letters adjacent to the capital are to be used.

With <u>ring</u> *removed from* <u>port</u>, Ed~~ward~~ /\ **showed indignation** (8)
  = Bristl**ed**

Remarkable <u>detail Pop</u> *produced, without* <u>hesitation</u> /, of\
  butterflies and moths (11) = Lepidoptera

<u>Rome</u> *was rebuilt in* <u>my</u> /\ **recollection** (6) = Memor**y**

Man /\ <u>is</u> *back before* <u>Mon~~day~~</u> (5) = **Si**mon

<u>Doctor</u> *coming from* <u>Oslo</u> /\ **shows gushing appreciation** (6)
  = Drools

Unfriendly /\ <u>Alf~~red~~</u> *goes round* <u>the ducks</u> (5) = A**loof**

Single /\ <u>principle</u> <u>Ray</u> *manipulated* (10) = Elementa**ry**

Banish /\ <u>the peasant</u> *at* E~~yemouth~~ (9) = Rusticate

<u>Stan~~ley-Church~~</u> *and* <u>I operating</u> /\ **the bar** (9) = Stan**chion**

Never /coming from\ ~~North~~ <u>Ayr</u> *resort* (4) = N**ary**

<u>Con~~stance and~~ Den~~ise~~</u> *I leave* /\ **make it briefer** (8) = Con**dense**

<u>By Al~~an~~</u> *shortly performing* /\ **skilfully** (4) = **Ably** (anagram)

Delicate surgery /–\ <u>yet Dr isn't</u> *involved!* (9) = Dentistry (anagram)

Sculptor /\ <u>Ron~~ald~~</u> *embracing* <u>Dia~~na~~</u> (5) = Rodin (concon)

<u>CD nearly</u> *damaged* /–\ **use solvent to remove dirt** (3-5) = **D**ry-clean

<u>W~~est~~ Wensleyd~~ale~~</u> *out of* <u>beer</u>, *surprisingly* /,\ for **the happy**
  couple (5-4) = Newly-weds

APOSTROPHE OF ELISION

An apostrophe of elision (letters left out) often means that the letters around it need to be used in constructing the answer.

After the <u>legal document</u> *was issued,* <u>he'd</u> /\ **contorted as if in**
  pain (7) = Writh**ed**

<u>Counter</u> <u>'e'd</u> /\ **pushed about roughly** (8) = Buffeted

<u>I'm</u> *after* <u>a letter</u> /\ **written by Kipling** (3) = Kim

Another <u>cost</u> *on the* <u>ch~~urch~~ 'e'd</u> /\ **put an end to** (8) = Scot**ched**
  (buildword)

<u>Firm</u> <u>soil's</u> *been displaced* /by the\ **statues** (7) = **C**olossi

Surprised expression /\ <u>we</u> ~~will~~ *shortly repeat* (4,4) = Well well
  (We'll we'll. The apostrophe is indicated by the keyword
  'shortly')

More often than not an anagram is indicated.

Delicate surgery /–\ <u>yet Dr isn't</u> *involved!* (9) = Dentistry
Drunken <u>lady 'e</u> /\ **put off** (5) = Delay
<u>One isn't</u> *creating* /\ **a state of suspense** (7) = Tension
Irregular <u>tradin' I'd</u> /discovered\ **in the West Indies** (8) = Trinidad
Separate /\ <u>act he'd</u> *developed* (6) = Detach
<u>Joan I'd</u> *moved* /to be\ **next to** (6) = Adjoin
Military unit's /\ <u>barge I'd</u> *rebuilt* (7) = Brigade
<u>Rider, 'e'd</u> *upset* /\ **the girl** (7) = Deirdre
Fruit /\ <u>Irene can't</u> *remove* (9) = Nectarine
<u>Huron's</u> *producing* /\ **a forceful forward flow** (6) = Onrush
Gave a new heading /to\ <u>letter I'd</u> *rewritten* (8) = Retitled
<u>Let's wash lace in a</u> *new way*. /It must be\ **spotless** (5,2,1,7)
    = Clean as a whistle
<u>Can't a cross</u> *be arranged as* /being\ **the most sacred?** (10)
    = Sacrosanct
<u>Heater we'd</u> *removed* /had become\ **discoloured by exposure** (9)
    = Weathered
<u>Rene's</u> *upset* /by\ **expression of contempt** (5) = Sneer
<u>Cadi's</u> *mixing* /\ **sour substances** (5) = Acids
<u>Diana's</u> *replaced by another* /\ **woman** (5) = Nadia
Spendthrift /\ <u>Walter's</u> *reformed* (7) = Wastrel
<u>Patina's</u> *reapplied,* <u>majestically</u> /,\ **in meticulous style** (13)
    = Painsta**kingly**

The genitive apostrophe also usually points to an anagram.

<u>Hampton's</u> *weird* /\ **ghost** (7) = Phantom
<u>See Carol's</u> *recipe* /for\ **a hot dish** (9) = Casserole
One paid to work /in\ <u>tavern's</u> *restoration* (7) = Servant
<u>Mother's</u> *turn* /\ **to stifle** (7) = Smother
To show contempt /could be\ <u>Rene's</u> *undoing* (5) = Sneer
<u>Rene's</u> *turn* /to\ **show contempt** (5) = Sneer
When <u>Ian's aorta</u> *ruptured* he went into **one of these** (9)
    = Sanatoria
Crooked <u>NCO's</u> /\ **swindles** (4) = Cons

Abbreviation (Apostrophe of elision)

Reply /\ per Don's *order* (7) = Respond
Hoodlum /\ *upset* Gert's nag (8) = Gangster

JARGON
There are two broad categories of jargon: the jargon of other fields of expertise and the jargon that is peculiar to cryptic crosswords.

SPECIALIST JARGON FROM OTHER FIELDS
Horse racing
Eccentric boy? /\ **Sure thing!** (4,2) = Odds on

Golf
Last /\ but two, to score (10) = Eighteenth
A birdie or one better *in the* valleys /of\ **course** (10) = **Glen**eagles
Placing /\ on the green (7) = Putting
Skinhead drove off /on\ **a lively horse** (5) = Steed

Tennis
Note: Love lines /are\ **macabre** (9) = Gory (Love = 0)

Music
Looks /for\ a soft fruit (7) = Appears
Gently press /for\ **expulsions** (5) = **P**urge
A glider /is\ equally quiet (3) = Asp
Join /\ a very loud team (5) = Affix
(P is short for piano, meaning soft, and f is short for forte, loud.)
Note: Love lines /are\ macabre (9) = Gory (Love = 0)
Poet /\ writes note *held by disheartened* singer (7) = Spenser
(Notes are the letters a, b, c, d, e, f, g, h or Do re mi fa so la te doh.)
The man /\ coming to a stop (4) = Adam
(M is for Musette, an organ stop.)
Oh dear! /–\ nothing works (4) = Oops
(Opus is Latin for work. Op is its abbreviation, singular, a work.
Magnum opus = Great work. Ops = works, plural.)

Heraldry
Respecting a black *holding* on /, as is\ **quite right** (10) = Reason**able**

Military
Female ∧ soldiers *after* company (4) = Co**ra**
Combatant *holding* regiment *in* /a\ **cargo vessel!** (9) = Freighter

Numismatics
Head /of\ old British lines? (7) = Ob**verse**

Latin
The man ∧ coming to a stop (4) = **Ad**am
He has been instructed to vote ∧ for two unknowns (5) = **Pro**xy
Type of recorder /on which\ to see nothing ! (5) = **Vide**o

Algebra
He has been instructed to vote ∧ for two unknowns (5) = Pro**xy**

Classical allusion
Peter right *inside* the church /will\ **swagger** (6) = Pr**an**ce (Peter Pan)

Geography
Transatlantic writers *in* the Home Counties /generate\ **excitement**
  (8) = **Sus**pense (Transatlantic = us and Home Counties =
  SE. A good condix.)

Macaroni
And *in France* learn *about* /it being\ **everlasting** (7) = **Et**ernal
Wants *to be out of* the *French* ∧ **sewers** (7) = Need**les**

JARGON PECULIAR TO CRYPTIC CROSSWORDS
Mail *distributed round* a point ∧ **in Africa** (6) = Malawi
Break *at* quarter *past* four ∧ **feeling fidgety** (7) = Restive
(Compass points, or quarters, are the cardinal points, North,
South, East, West.)
Reports /from\ all quarters (4) = News
From north-east, Augustus /brought\ **hot wine** (5) = Negus

3. Devices Used to Reconstruct Clues into Answers

Circle an island /\ **sultanate** (4) = **O**man
Oh dear! /–\ ~~nothing~~ works (4) = **O**ops
Vegetarian Circle's /\ **celebration?** (5) = Bean**o**
Harry /\ can be a fearsome beast *with* ~~nothing~~ *inside him* (7)
    = Drag**o**on
In archaelogical excavation, ~~name~~ worker /\ **showing scorn** (9)
    = In**dign**ant
Illusory hope /\ of painter wearing black tie? (7) = **Ra**inbow
    (Painter = Royal Academician = RA)
Portentous /\ doctor *lifted* one *with* common sense (7) =
    Ominous (Doctor = DD, Dr, GP, MB, MD, MO)
Note: Love lines /are\ **macabre** (9) = G**o**ry (Love = 0)
Lines are railway lines, abbreviated to Ry. Elsewhere lines are lines
of poetry.
Head of ~~old British~~ lines? (7) = Ob**verse**
Setting out, steer ship *inside* /\ **locks** (7) = Tre**ss**es
Bill *and* Edward *got* out of bed /and\ **behaved badly** (5,2) = Ac**ted**
    up (Bill is an account, ac. William is Bill and Edward is Ted.)

The -er suffix is important because it is often used. One who sews
is a sewer. That which has banks is a banker, like the river Dee.
That which flows is a flower and that which blooms is a bloomer.

Wants *to be out of* the *French* /\ **sewers** (7) = **Need**les
Put out of order /,\ called *in the* banker (7) = **De**range
European flower /with\ *utterly* distinctive smell (4) = Oder
Nora *Batty* /,\ **flower of Italy?** (4) = Arno
Flower round a lot of yards /is\ **a tea plant** (8) = **Cam**omile
Film /\ Caledonian flower (7) = Pict**ure**
I backed Ru *wrongly* /producing\ a **bloomer** (9) = Rudbeckia

The jargon of cryptic crosswords is an unbelievably vast field of
study, on which several books have already been published. The
field is so vast that even the best crossword dictionaries cannot
cope with the extensive duplication required for adequate cross-
referencing. See, for example, *The Complete Crossword
Companion* by Jeremy Howard-Williams (1997. Harper Collins

Publishers, London). The selection below is intended to give a further glimpse into the field and to give a further idea of what is meant by crossword jargon and how the jargon is abbreviated to dixes.

<u>Lets</u> *out* <u>American</u> *imprisoned in* /\ **brawl** (6) = Tus**s**le (Condix)
Drinking-party /\ <u>song</u> *about* <u>America</u> (8) = Carou**sa**l (Condix)
<u>Sappers</u> *in* <u>aircraft</u> /,\ **a transporter** (9) = F**re**ighter (Condix) (RE = Royal Engineers)
<u>Engineers</u> *circling* <u>at</u> /\ **speed** (4) = Ra**t**e (Condix) (RE = Royal Engineers)
Noble lady /is\ <u>unrivalled</u>, *but without* <u>money</u> (7) = Pe**er**ess (Disheartenment) (L, s, d = Money. Also p = penny.)
Temple /of\ <u>deity</u> *ringed by* <s>parking</s> <u>motorists</u> (6) = Pa**go**da (Buildword) (AA = Automobile Association)
Antagonist /\ <u>these days</u> <u>raves</u> *about* <s>railway</s> (9) = **Ad**versary (Buildword) (Ry = Railway. AD = Anno Domini.)
<u>Exercises</u> *absorbing* <u>very large</u> /\ **model** (4) = Po**s**e (Condix) (OS = outsize. PE = Physical Exercise)
<u>A firm</u> <u>supporter</u> /, but\ **a crawler** (5) = Co**bra** (Co = Company)
May appear <u>alert</u>, *with* <u>craft</u> /or\ **without craft** (7) = Artle**ss** (SS = Steam Ship, Sailing Ship)

NUMERS
Numers are an interesting way of abbreviating numerical information given in the clue. Numers are discussed at length later, but here are a few examples to illustrate the phenomenon as it applies to abbreviation.

<u>Pat</u><s>rick</s> *returns before* <u>ten</u>, *it appears, with* <u>accountant</u> /for\ **some starchy food** (7) = Ta**pi**oca
<u>50</u>-1 <u>odds</u> /in\ **a manner of speaking** (4) = **Li**sp
Fancy /\ *taking* <u>off</u> *without* <u>one!</u> (6) = Notion (not within!)
Acid /\ number <u>six thousand three hundred and fifty</u> (7) = Vi**tri**ol (VI + Trio + L = 6 + 3 + 50. From 6350)
Acid /\ number 6350 = Vi**tri**ol
635,099 = Vitriolic (Vi trio l ic)

ELEMENTS

The periodic table of chemical elements has a well known set of abbreviations.

Drawback /using\ tin *with* silver (4) = **Sn**ag
Pierced /\ *different* kind *with* iron (6) = Kni**fe**d
Place /\ silicon *in a* medicinal drink (8) = Po**si**tion
Writer /of\ The God *with the Crown of* Gold (6) = **Au**thor

Parabrebit

> Parabrebit is a contraction of 'paraphrase and abbreviate to a bitword'. The chief requirement is that the result of the operation is no more than three letters long. The resultant abbreviation and paraphrase need not necessarily be a word itself, but can be a dix.

Things *broadcast about* American /\ **electioneering** (8) = Hus**t**ings
In the morning, corny *sort* /of\ **word formed from initials** (7)
    = a**cronym**
Ridicule /\ *the French* member *having* ~~nothing~~ on (7) = Lamp**oon**
Book *a* turn /\ **in New Zealand** (5) = **Ot**ago

US, am, MP and OT are abbreviations, but not of the words American, morning, member and book. An element of paraphrasing has been introduced to complement the abbreviation. These examples are not mere abbreviations, but have also been paraphrased to some extent. Straightforward abbreviations abound in crosswords and are not to be confused with parabrebits.

Marsupial /to\ ~~knock out~~ the boy *almost* (5) = **Ko**ala
Famous /\ ~~name~~ now *scrambled in a* rush (8) = Renowned
Doctor *coming from* Oslo /\ **shows gushing appreciation** (6)
    = **Dr**ools
Spade /in\ ~~second~~ hut (6) = **S**hovel
It is muddy /\ on the ~~second~~ green (5) = **S**lime

The distinctions between an abbreviation, an initial and a parabrebit are not always very clear. Obviously many recognised abbreviations are the initials of the words they stand for, but crosswords use many initials that are not recognised abbreviations. What distinguishes the parabrebit is the latitude taken in paraphrasing before abbreviating. The ideal parabrebit is easy to distinguish from the abbreviation or the initial because of the paraphrasing:

Change course /\ *when the* <u>vessel</u>*'s caught in the* <u>swell</u> (4,3)
  = **Turn** off
<u>The</u> *French* <u>travel</u> <u>on</u> /\ **the lake** (6) = La**go**on
A <u>fool</u> *with* <u>a</u> /\ **girl** (5) = A**nit**a
Trouble /\ *has surrounded* <u>Abyssinian prince</u> (6) = Ha**rass**
<u>No</u> <u>approval</u> /for\ **retreat** (4) = N**ook**
<u>Vessel</u> I ~~caught~~ /in\ **terror** (5) = **Pan**ic
A glider /is\ <u>equally</u> <u>quiet</u> (3) = **As**p
In <u>archaelogical excavation</u>, ~~name~~ <u>worker</u> /\ **showing scorn** (9)
  = In**dign**ant

The above examples have been paraphrased and shortened to bitwords, but the next examples were first paraphrased and then abbreviated to form dixes, which are not bitwords because they are not words.

Offensive /\ <u>rumour</u> *about a retired* <u>doctor</u> (7) = No**iso**me
<u>50</u>-<u>1</u> <u>odds</u> /in\ **a manner of speaking** (4) = Li**sp**
~~Young~~ *leader* <u>Bill</u> *had* <u>night</u> *out* /\ **sailing** (8) = Ya**ch**ting
<u>Firm</u> <u>soil's</u> *been displaced by the* /\ **statues** (7) = **Co**lossi
A <u>group of sailors</u> <u>love</u> /being\ ~~on~~ **the river** (4) = Arno

There is a diversity of ways in which words and phrases are reduced to only a few letters.

NUMER
After false <u>alarm</u> <u>one</u> *receives* <u>a</u> /\ **complaint** (7) = Malaria
~~Patrick~~ *returns before* <u>ten</u> *it appears, with* <u>accountant</u> /for\ **some starchy food** (7) = Ta**pio**ca

Sticky ∧ <u>heavy soil</u> *contains* <u>thousands</u> (6) = Cla**mm**y

MACARONI
Sort out ∧ <u>a</u> *Parisian* <u>quintet</u> *in* <u>real</u> *trouble* (7) = **Un**ravel

JARGON
Spread ∧ <u>ruin</u> – <u>got</u> *about* <u>a</u> <u>pound</u> (9) = Mar**ma**lade (Mar + a £ inside made)
<u>Old Bob</u> <u>raced</u> *about* ∧ **frightened** (6) = **S**cared

CLASSICAL ALLUSION
<u>Peter</u> ~~right~~ *inside* the <u>church</u> /will\ **swagger** (6) = **Pr**ance

GEOGRAPHY
<u>Transatlantic</u> <u>writer</u> *in the* <u>Home Counties</u> /generates\ **excitement** (8) = **Sus**pense
<u>Corner</u> <u>a</u> <u>team</u> /at the\ **holiday resort** (7) = **Se**aside
<u>Everybody</u>, <u>say</u>, *with* <u>alternative</u> I <u>state</u> /to be\ **symbolic** (11) = Allegori**cal**

LATIN
He lets loose /and is\ <u>about</u> *to* <u>curse</u> *badly* (7) = **Re**scuer
Oh dear! /–\ ~~nothing~~ <u>works</u> (4) = O**ops**

MILITARY JARGON
<u>Hon</u>~~ourable~~ <u>theologian</u> *taken in by* <u>gunners</u> /in\ **Welsh valley** (7) = **R**hondd**a**

HUMER
Portentous ∧ <u>doctor</u> *lifted* <u>one</u> *with* <u>common sense</u> (7) = **Om**inous
Illusory hope /of\ <u>painter</u> <u>wearing</u> <u>black tie</u>? (7) = **Ra**inbow
Agreeing /with\ <u>many</u> <u>over</u> <u>boy</u> <u>worker</u> (9) = Conson**ant**
Washstand /that's\ <u>oval</u> *surprisingly* <u>sailor</u> *included* (6) = Lava**bo**

Most parabrebits are first paraphrased and then abbreviated.

Book	Old Testament	OT
Book	New Testament	NT
Morning	Ante Meridiem	AM
Nowadays	Anno Domini	AD
Gunners	Royal Artillery	RA
State	California	Cal
Sailor	Able Seaman	AB
Corner	South East	SE
Home Counties	South East	SE
Old Bob	Shilling	S
Hundred	Centum	C
Thousand	Mille	M
Painter	Royal Academician	RA
Group of sailors	Royal Navy	RN
Odds	Starting Price	SP
Bill	Account	Ac
Firm	Company	Co
Doctor	Medical Officer	MO
Doctor	General Practitioner	GP
Doctor	Doctor of Divinity	DD
Doctor	Doctor of Philosophy	PhD
Doctor	Medicinae Baccalaureus	MB
Doctor	Medicinae Doctor	MD
Doctor	Bachelor of Medicine	BM

Parabreve

Parabreve means to paraphrase and abbreviate, but not to a bitword. It is important to bear this in mind because of the constant tendency to shorten the words in the clue, and because of the constant quest for short words. One must learn to think in short words first; only when they fail should one start to seek long words.

Brazilian footballer *on the way up* has *included* book /of\ **large animals** (9) = **Elep**hants

Parabreve

Buy stock ∧ <u>in</u> <u>clothes</u> (6) = In**vest**
Do well ∧ with <u>professional</u> <u>representatives</u>' *back-up* (7) = Pro**sper**
Found out how many ∧ *frolicking* <u>deer</u> *were* <u>unable to move</u> *for a start* (8) = **Numb**ered
<u>I speak maliciously</u> /about the\ **inhabitant** (8) = I**slander**
Inattentive ∧ <u>Nigel</u> *confused* <u>the fellow</u> (9) = Negli**gent**
Malevolent ∧ <u>prince</u> *loosely* <u>promises to pay</u> (10) = Pernic**ious**
<u>Patina's</u> *re-applied,* <u>majestically</u> /,\ **in meticulous style** (13) = Painsta**kingly**
Perceiving ∧ <u>no</u> <u>sound</u> (6) = Not**ing**
<u>Reveals</u> *another* <u>sound</u> ∧ **that goes on and on** (11) = Everlas**ting**
Roguish ∧ <u>associate</u> *smashed* <u>cars</u> *first* (8) = Rasc**ally**
Single ∧ <u>composer</u> *reversing* <u>usual function</u> (8) = Bach**elor**
Stop ∧ <u>record</u> on *other* <u>unit,</u> <u>fifth rate</u> (11) = **Disc**ontinue
<u>The</u> <u>restraint</u> /apparent\ **inside** (7) = The**rein**

See Paraphrase on page 96.

Anagram

> When the anagram is used as a device it can mean that *some* of the letters in the answer are transposed from the clue in the construction of another type of clue's answer.

ANAGRAM IN A BUILDWORD
Vessel ∧ *almost* <u>departed</u> *with the wrong* <u>load</u> (7) = Gon**dola**
Spanish nobleman ∧ <u>concealed</u> <u>gaol</u>*break* (7) = Hid**algo**
Top commander ∧ <u>to drink</u> <u>more</u> – *getting drunk* (7) = Sup**remo**
<u>At home</u> *breaks* <u>leg</u> /on\ **fireplace** (5) = In**gle**
<u>Writer</u> <u>suing</u> *odd* ∧ **underwater swimmers** (8) = **Pen**guins
Relating to land /in\ <u>Indian city</u> *before* <u>rain</u>-*storm* (8) = Agra**rian**
Surrender to another country ∧ <u>additional</u> <u>diet</u> *ingredients* (9) = Extra**dite**
<u>One</u> *maybe* <u>according to reason</u> ∧ **concerned with new works** (10) = **Neo**logical
Guilty person ∧ <u>rode</u> *off but* <u>not in the right way</u> *to start with* (9) = Wrong**doer**

<u>Wave</u> *after* <u>awl</u> *had been damaged by* ∧ **a criminal** (10)
= **Law**breaker

CONDIX IN AN ANAGRAM
Remarkable <u>detail Pop</u> *produced, without* <u>hesitation</u> /,\ of
butterflies and moths (11) = Lepidoptera
Setting out, <u>steer</u> <u>ship</u> *inside* ∧ **locks** (7) = Tresses
<u>Hurried</u> *in* <u>most</u> *upset about* ∧ **a lintel** (7) = Transom
Later ∧ *rebuilt* <u>raft</u> *going round* <u>the orient</u> (5) = **Aft**er
Calmed ∧ <u>amateur</u> *during new* <u>deal</u> (7) = **All**ay**ed**
<u>Can't</u> *change* <u>quantity of money</u> *going round* ∧ **holy place** (7)
= **Sanct**um
Peculiar <u>charm</u> *of* <u>a</u> <u>threesome</u> *endlessly held by* ∧ **an old
woman of great dignity** (9) = **M**at**riarch** (triad)
<u>Rome</u> *was rebuilt in* <u>my</u> ∧ **recollection** (6) = **Mem**ory
Give up hope /of\ *bumpy* <u>ride</u> *around the* <u>resort</u> (7) = **Des**pair
Having been brought up ∧ *in* <u>ancient city,</u> *turned* <u>wild</u> (8)
= **N**ur**tured**
<u>Tries</u> *somehow* <u>to take food</u> *inside* /during\ **work** (8) = Treatise

PHRASE
Is content with present achievements /,\ <u>reason nurse let loss</u>
deteriorate (5,2,4,7) = Rests on one's laurels
Successful people in it *suffering* <u>total non-reality</u>? (8,7) =
National Lottery

ABBREVIATION
<u>Taxmen</u> *in another* <u>capital</u> ∧ **practising robbery at sea!** (9)
= Piratical
<u>Lets</u> *out* <u>American</u> *imprisoned in* ∧ **brawl** (6) = Tussle
Antique type /,\ <u>for example</u> – <u>painty</u> *sort* (8) = **Eg**yptian

CURTAILMENT AND UNDIX
<u>Were</u> *endlessly about to leave* <u>the wrong</u> ∧ **strap** (5) = Thong

TRANSDELETION
<u>No record</u> *endlessly arranged* /for the\ **singer** (7) = Crooner

Anagram

MACARONI
Eric *going wild about* <u>the</u> *French* ∧ **girl** (6) = Claire

NUMER
After false <u>alarm</u> <u>one</u> *receives* <u>a</u> ∧ **complaint** (7) = Malaria
Terrible <u>actors</u> took <u>99</u> /attempts at\ **the word puzzle** (8) = Acrostic
Uncommon things ∧ *produced by* <u>eleven</u> *in* <u>arrest</u>, *perhaps* (8)
   = Rarities

CAPITAL LETTERS
Banded appearance of rocks /caused by\ <u>early</u> *movement* <u>in</u>
G~~reek~~ *capital* (8) = **Layer**ing

Apostrophe

> An apostrophe (A comma over a space left by missing letters)
> in the clue usually means that the letters around the apostrophe
> need to be used to construct the answer.

ELISION

> Elision is a literary device by which a vowel or syllable is
> omitted from a word in pronouncing. The omission is usually
> marked by an apostrophe when written, but crossword answer
> grids do not assign a square for the apostrophe or draw
> attention to it in any way when it occurs in an answer.

Irregular <u>tradin' I'd</u> /discovered\ **in the West Indies** (8) = Trinidad
Another <u>cost</u> *on the* <u>ch~~urch~~ 'e'd</u> ∧ **put an end to** (8) = Scotched
U~~niversity~~ <u>trainin'</u> *a new* ∧ **believer** (9) = Unitarian
Separate ∧ <u>act he'd</u> *developed* (6) = Detach
<u>One isn't</u> *creating* ∧ **a state of suspense** (7) = Tension
<u>Ben's no fraternal</u> *kind* ∧ **that cannot be passed on** (3-12) = Non-
   transferable
<u>Rene's</u> *upset* /by\ **expression of contempt** (5) = Sneer

Elision may be required en route to the answer.

Fancy <u>sweet</u> ~~had~~ *shortly* /been\ **cooked slowly**! (6) = Stew**ed**
Most of <u>time</u>, <u>I</u> ~~would~~ /\ **appear shy** (5) = Tim**id**
<u>But</u> *in retreat* <u>I</u> ~~have~~ /to be\ **devious** (7) = Evasive

POSSESSION
The apostrophe of possession almost always indicates an anagram.

Crooked <u>NCO's</u> /\ **swindles** (4) = Cons
<u>Then city's</u> *production* /is\ **artificially produced** (9) = Synthetic

An apostrophe of possession may be required in the answer.

Is content with present achievements /,\ <u>reason nurse let loss</u>
   deteriorate (5,2,4,7) = Rests on one's laurels

Bitword

A bitword is a word of less than four letters.

Cryptic crosswords depend greatly on the use of bitwords. It is because English is so rich in bitwords that the game is more suitable to English than any other language. There are two sources of bitwords: those already in the clue, and those that are deduced from longer words in the clue. Bitwords already in the clue are used in almost every type of clue.

ANAGRAM
Power /–\ <u>mains at</u> *exchange* (7) = Stamina
<u>The cards</u> *might be* /made\ **stiffer** (8) = Starched
The protection /of\ <u>cod takes</u> *organisation* (8) = Stockade
<u>Rat must</u> *emerge from* /\ **the rock layer** (7) = Stratum
New <u>trains,</u> *about* <u>ten</u> /,\ **staying only a short time** (9) = Transient
Coming from <u>port shop I</u> *made* /for\ **the boat** (9) = Troopship
<u>Let my tape</u> *get twisted round* /\ **an alloy** (4-5) = Type-metal

BRIDGEWORD

A sti~~ll~~ *starting to produce* /\ **wine** (4) = Asti
Indian nurse /\ *from* ~~Bomb~~ay – a h~~ard worker~~ (4) = Ayah
Wanting some ~~grub,~~ I stro~~de~~ /into\ **café** (6) = Bistro
Fish /\ *in the* ~~shop a h~~ake~~?~~ (4) = Opah
In ~~chapel is se~~lf ~~conscious~~ /wearing this\ **cloak** (7) = Pelisse
Wild-fowl /\ *in* ~~qui~~te a ~~large reserve~~ (4) = Teal

CONCON

Lay /\ feeling under the weather – all *in* (6) = **Ball**ad
Lower /\ churchman *embraces* me (6) = **Deme**an
Mia *takes* girl *inside* /some\ **medicinal powder** (8) = **Magnes**ia
Mum *goes round* a mark left /by\ **make-up** (7) = **Mascar**a
Position *protecting* a /\ **large building** (6) = **Palac**e
Fruit /\ is *gathered in* the fall (6) = **Rais**in
One frequenting /\ a section Hugh *is said to have gone round* (7)
    = **Habitué**
Charlie *embraces* a /\ **padre** (8) = Chaplain
Did *go round* ~~southern~~ gatehouse /,\ **having been evicted** (9)
    = Dis**lodge**d
Refuse /\ to see habitual joker *included* (6) = Se**wag**e

SPLITWORD

A piece of ammunition /\ **near at hand** (6) = A**round**
Illegal act /\ of a guard (7) = **Off**ence
A footballer *taken thus* /\ **by surprise** (5) = A**back**
A footballer *taken thus* /is\ **disconcerted** (5) = A**back**
A cat /has\ **a very small part** (4) = A**tom**
A number assume /it to be\ **fibrous tissue** (6) = Ten**don**

BUILDWORD

A person facing the truth /\ about a heel (7) = Realist
After an alcoholic drink, a /\ **pain in the chest** (6) = Angin**a**
Again choose /\ dance etc. *arrangement* (2-5) = Re-el**ect**
Birds /\ model it *in* the football team (8) = Blue**tit**s
After the legal document *was issued,* he'd /\ **contorted as if in**
    pain (7) = Writ**hed**

Remains *with* one I left /\ **found on the boat** (8) = Staysail
I'm *after* a letter /\ **written by Kipling** (3) = Kim

REVERSALS
After talk, let's *return* /\ **property** (7) = Chattel
Stuffing not *replaced* /on\ **bear** (10) = Paddington

BACKWORDS
Not *backed* /\ **much** (5) = Ton

CONDIX
The outlook /for\ coppers *brought into* a division (6) = Aspect
Do *include,* these days /,\ **a deep border of wood** (4) = Dado
In the country *head of* house is /\ **right to vote** (9) = Franchise
Her wager *is about* right /for\ **a man** (7) = Herbert

Bitwords deduced from longer words in the clue.

ABBREVIATION
Minor cleric /\ *needs* a *little* company *in the* study (6) = Deacon
Lets *out* American *imprisoned in* /\ **brawl** (6) = Tussle (Condix)
Drinking-party /\ song *about* America (8) = Carousal (Condix)
Antagonist /\ these days raves *about* railway (9) = **Ad**versary
Exercises *absorbing* very large /\ **model** (4) = Pose (Condix)
A firm supporter /, but\ **a crawler** (5) = Cobra
May appear alert, *with* craft /or\ **without craft** (7) = Artless
   (SS = steam ship)

HOMOPHONE
Girl /has\ a large drink *as stated* (7) = Abigail
Lynne *reportedly holds* up /\ **a garden flower** (5) = Lupin
One frequenting /\ a section Hugh *is said to have gone round* (7)
   = Habitué

HUMER
Advances /\ **a member of the family** (7) = Stepson
Archdeacon *accepts* nearly ten /from\ **a spiteful woman** (5) = Vixen

Bitword (Humer)

Sculptor /\ ~~Ron~~ald *embracing* ~~Di~~ana (5) = Rodin
From ~~north-east,~~ Augustus /brought\ **hot wine** (5) = Ne**gus**
A spinner *at his* /\ **peak?** (4) = A**top**
Auditor /perhaps\ hired Bill to tell *the* worker (9,10) = Chartered
accountant
Coloured /\ worker *in* transport (7) = Slanted

JARGON
Circle an island /\ **sultanate** (4) = Oman
Oh dear! /–\ ~~nothing~~ works (4) = Oops
Vegetarian Circle's /\ **celebration?** (5) = Beano
Harry /can be\ a fearsome beast *with* ~~nothing~~ *inside him* (7)
= Drag**oon**
Put out of order /,\ called *in the* banker (7) = De**range**
Flower round a lot of yards /is\ **a tea plant** (8) = Cam**omile**
Film /\ Caledonian flower (7) = Picture

LATIN
The man /\ coming to a stop (4) = Ad**am**
Respecting a black *holding* on /, as is\ **quite right** (10) = Re**asonable**
Oh dear! /–\ ~~nothing~~ works (4) = Oops
He has been instructed to vote /\ for two unknowns (5) = Pro**xy**

MACARONI
Who *in France in the* ~~east~~ calling /for\ **the misleading use of
doubtful words?** (12) = Equi**vocation**
Ridicule /\ *the French* member *having* ~~nothing~~ on (7) = La**mpoon**
The *French* travel on /\ **the lake** (6) = La**goon**
Alight /\ from *French* coaches (7) = De**train**
Territory /\ *of the French* ~~church~~ unknown (5) = Du**chy**
Eric *going wild about* the *French* /\ **girl** (6) = Claire (Condix)
~~Exiting~~ *start made by* five *in French* street /to produce\ **theatrical
work** (5) = Revue (Condix)
A *French* oil painting ~~perhaps~~ /, it is\ **banal** (10) = Un**original**
(Buildword)
The *French going in* for /\ **alcoholic liquor** (4) = Ales (Concon)
Wants *to be out of* the *French* /\ **sewers** (7) = Need**les** (Concon)

Bitword (Macaroni)

Shock ∧ <u>with reference to</u> *German* <u>conjunction</u> (7) = Asto**und**
Reprove ∧ <u>Scotsman</u> *embraced by* <u>a</u> <u>stunning</u> <u>looker</u> (8) = Ad**mon**ish
<u>Day-dreaming</u> *about Spanish* <u>urging</u> ∧ **patience** (9) = T**ole**rance
<u>The</u> *Spanish* <u>porter</u> /has\ **to hang on** (4,3) = **Last** out

NUMER
<u>51</u> /and\ **single** (4) = **Lone**
<u>Alternative</u> *number first by* ∧ **a singer** (5) = **Ten**or
<u>A number</u> <u>assume it to be</u> ∧ **fibrous tissue** (6) = **Ten**don
<u>Small number</u> <u>at</u> ∧ **Welsh resort** (5) = **Ten**by
Bother ∧ <u>any</u> <u>small number</u> *inside* (5) = An**noy**
<u>Many</u> <u>arrived</u> *first* /at\ **legendary English town** (7) = Came**lot**

PARABREBIT
Doubly <u>evil</u> ∧ **sailor** (6) = Sin**bad**
<u>Girl</u> <u>able to</u> *recall* ∧ **a whole lot of dates** (7) = Alma**nac**
Change course ∧ *when the* <u>vessel</u>'s *caught in the* <u>swell</u> (4,3) =
    T**urn** off
<u>The</u> *French* <u>travel</u> <u>on</u> ∧ **the lake** (6) = lago**on**
<u>A</u> <u>fool</u> *with* <u>a</u> ∧ **girl** (5) = An**ita**
Trouble ∧ <u>has</u> *surrounded* <u>Abyssinian prince</u> (6) = Ha**rass**
<u>No</u> <u>approval</u> /for\ **retreat** (4) = N**ook**
<u>Vessel</u> <u>I caught</u> /in\ **terror** (5) = P**anic**
A glider /is\ <u>equally</u> <u>quiet</u> (3) = **Asp**
<u>In</u> <u>archaeological excavation</u>, <u>name</u> <u>worker</u> ∧ **showing scorn** (9)
    = In**dign**ant

UNDIX
<u>Professional</u> <u>examination</u> /giving rise to\ **complaint** (7) = Pro**test**
From <u>north-east, Augustus</u> /brought\ **hot wine** (5) = Ne**gus**
Agenda /for\ <u>education</u> *in* <u>German school</u> (8) = Sche**dule**
<u>Open land</u> *at both ends of* <u>Langley</u>, **generally** (8) = Common**ly**
One follows ∧ <u>smash-hit</u> *with* <u>operational-research</u> (9) = Success**or**
<u>Said</u> *before second half of* <u>July</u> ∧ **in the appointed manner** (8)
    = Stated**ly**
Clearly /but\ <u>lazily</u> *having most of the* <u>luck</u> *first* (7) = Luci**dly**
She ∧ *gets the same bit of* <u>luck</u> *twice* (4) = Lu**lu**
Pouch /makes up\ *most of the* <u>large bag</u> (3) = Sac (sa**ck**)

Reversal

A reversal occurs when some or all the letters of a word are used in their reverse order in the construction of the answer, but so that they do not make a word by themselves. A word that becomes another word when used backwards is a backword, and a backword that remains unchanged when reversed is a palindrome.

An entrance /\ I'd *turn in* at (4) = A**dit**
Given to /, *back-*~~street~~ **youngsters** (4) = To**ts**
Man /\ is *back before* Mon~~day~~ (5) = **Si**mon
Tom *returns* /by alternative form of\ **transport** (5) = **Mot**or
Girl, able /to recall a\ **whole lot of dates** (7) = Alma**nac**
Retiring city, politician /gets\ **behind** (4) = **Ru**mp

The keywords for reversals are often direction sensitive, requiring down or across clues.

Letter from Greece /\ is *sent up, with a* note, *to* mother (5) = **Si**gma
Attract /\ father *bringing up.* ring (6) = **Ap**peal
The scholar /takes\ ages *to* sum *up* (7) = Eras**mus**
It *turns up, after* an /\ **opponent** (4) = An**ti**
Ron~~ald~~ *in* court *bringing up tips* /for\ the **waiters** (5) = Tron**c**
Travel *westwards on the* heather /\ **casting amorous glances** (6)
    = **Og**ling

4. Nonconstruction Devices

Cognation

> In cryptic crossword terminology cognate means related in meaning, not related by descent or through origin or derivation. Cognation is a nicety in the setting of crosswords. It has no function other than to impress andor please.

<u>Hits</u> *back* /in\ **fight** (4) = Spar (Raps)
<u>Hit</u> *back* /with\ a **whip** (4) = Taws (Swat)
<u>Propose</u> *motion*? /\ **He would do the converse** (7) = Opposer
Instruments of war /\ *from* <u>Mars</u> (4) = Arms
Mars, the god of war, yields two cognate anagrams: Arms and Rams.

Sometimes an anagram depends on the clue for the context that makes it cognate:

Tolerant philosophy /\ *confounded* <u>all evident evil</u> (4,3,3,4)
     = Live and let live
Lake /\ *formed when* <u>river rose</u> *dangerously* (9) = Reservoir
This old timer /\ *won't run* in <u>dry places</u> (9) = Clepsydra

Ellipsis

> Ellipsis is the omission from a sentence of words needed to complete construction or sense. It is characterised by the style of so many clues that appear to have been generated as SMS text messages. Setters use ellipsis to guide or to disguise.

Figure /\ of eight (7) = Octagon
(~~Geometric~~) **Figure** /\ of eight (~~equal sides and eight equal angles~~)
     (7) = Octagon
When bulbs come to life? (4) = Dusk

Ellipsis

When (light) bulbs come to life? (4) = Dusk
Not a friendly state (6) = Enmity
Not a friendly state (of relationship) (6) = Enmity
Bank of Scotland (4) = Brae
(River) Bank of Scotland (4) = Brae
Stern guide (6) = Rudder
Stern guide (on a boat) (6) = Rudder

Missing articles or prepositions are useful indicators of anagrams. Very often words normally used in ordinary sentence construction need to be omitted, lest they impede an anagram by becoming part of the exposition.

~~University~~ trainin' a *new* /\ **believer** (9) = Unitarian
The verb is incomplete to the extent that it does not even indicate tense (… is, was or will be trainin'?). This example is a buildword that uses an anagram as a device, and the bitword, 'a', conspicuously indicates the need for stacking and anagramming.

<u>Can veto</u> *conversion* /into\ **foreign currency** (7) = Centavo
The clue lacks a subject that would be present in normal sentence construction. The subject would do nothing but impede the anagram, so it has been omitted.

Geograph

> The geograph is a device in which solving clues depends on some geographical information or knowledge.

Suit /\ <u>I</u> *found in* <u>Ealing area</u> (6) = **Action**
The main road /from\ <u>home counties</u>, <u>abroad</u> (6) = **Se**away
<u>Walk</u>, *say* /,\ **the Russian plain** (6) = Steppe
The said <u>school members</u> /are in\ **the country** (5) = Wales
<u>A snug</u> *resort* /in\ **eastern Scotland** (5) = Angus
<u>A purge</u> *upsetting* /the\ **city** (6) = Prague
<u>A suit in</u> *material right* /for\ **a hot country** (7) = Tunisia

<u>Daimonic</u> *disruption* /\ **in the West Indies** (8) = Dominica
They're <u>settled collectively</u> in Israel (9) = Kibbutzim

Halph

> Halph is a contraction of '**hal**f a **ph**rase', since it refers to the clue in which only half of a phrase is given and the other half is needed to construct the answer.

Birds /\ <u>model</u> it *in* <u>the football team</u> (8) = Bluetits (Model T Ford)
<u>Charlie</u> *embraces* <u>a</u> /\ **padre** (8) = Chaplain (Charlie Chaplin)
Bear /to be\ <u>a hindu ascetic!</u> (4) = Yogi (Yogi Bear)
<u>Plainly she's a disaster</u> (8,4) = Calamity Jane (Plain Jane)
One having nine tenths of the law (9) = Possessor (Possession is nine tenths of the law)
Attractive /\ <u>tape</u> (8) = Magnetic (Magnetic tape)
Duck /\ <u>down</u> (5) = Eider (Eider down)
King /\ <u>penguin</u>? (7) = Emperor (Emperor Penguin)
Language /\ <u>school</u>? (7) = Grammar (Grammar school)
Festival /\ <u>season</u> (7) = Harvest (Harvest festival and harvest season)
Word /\ <u>case</u> (11) = Portmanteau (Portmanteau word)
Curvaceous /\ <u>Joan?</u> (3) = Arc (Joan of Arc)
<u>Peter,</u> *icy, say,* /causes\ **alarm** (5) = Panic (Peter Pan)
John /\ <u>of Orange?</u> (4) = Peel (John Peel and orange peel)
Odd /\ <u>street to be in when in debt</u> (5) = Queer (To be in Queer Street)
<u>Penny</u> ~~used to buy this~~ /\ **pipe** (7) = Whistle (Penny whistle)
<u>Jenny</u> /the\ **architect** (4) = Wren (Jenny wren and Sir Christopher Wren, the architect)

Homograph

> A homograph is a word spelled like another but different in meaning andor origin.

The homograph is important since it is the base of all paraphrasing from clue to answer. Remember that the homographic word has one meaning in the context of the clue (seen as a sentence) and another meaning that is used in the answer.

It is important to consider each word out of its context, since context often does no more than mislead.

Even weight /of\ **rock** (9) = **Iron**stone
Restrict ∧ studies *on* transport (9) = **Cons**train
Go *back into* Linden's ∧ **city** (7) = **Lim**oges
Do not leave ∧ **shore** (4) = Stay
Mis-hit ∧ **a boundary** (4) = Edge
A spill /,\ to come to the point (5) = Taper
Watches exercise /when there's\ **a problem in sight** (3-6)
    = **Eye-s**train
A stripper /in\ excellent physical shape (7) = Ace**tone**
Chief, *during the* theatrical performance /,\ had ~~some foreign~~
    money (7) = **Drachma**
Sappers *in* aircraft /,\ **a transporter** (9) = **Freight**er
Consume gin *in a* breather /from\ **hitting out** (7) = **Lung**ing
Confess *capturing* pawn /was\ **very bad** (8) = **Shock**ing
Russell *takes* Scotsman /to be\ **one from another country** (7)
    = **Russi**an
But not during the night, *two* ~~levers~~ *initially* ∧ **loiter** (5) = **Dally**

There are several helpful methods of paraphrasing the homograph:

PASOP

Look out for a misleading part of speech or confusing punctuation.

Neat /\ **barrier** /\ **on the way** (6-4) = Cattle-grid

Neat must be paraphrased as a noun. It is not an adjective.

Dreamers /who are\ thought heels (9) = **Idea**lists

Thought is a noun, not a verb. Heels is a verb, not a plural noun.

Being gross, a heel /\ **will take whatever comes** (8) = Fatalist

The separation of ideas does not occur at the comma, but after heel in the middle of a coherent phrase.

Setting out, steer ship *inside* /\ **locks** (7) = Tresses

Set out the letters of steer, and insert ship. The punctuation misleads.

SYNONYMTWIN

Stay /\ second (7) = Support

In this example support is a homograph and stay and second are synonymtwins of each other. They are not synonyms of each other, but are twins by virtue of having a common synonym, support.

PARABREBIT

In every cryptic crossword puzzle it will be necessary to paraphrase and abbreviate some words to bitwords, thus exploiting unusual homographic meanings of words. Bitwords are words of less than four letters.

Dismantle /a\ United Nations oil installation? (5) = Un**rig**

Spread /\ ruin – got *about* a pound (9) = **Mar**malade

Book a turn /\ **in New Zealand** (5) = Otago

Fall /of\ rotter *in* law-suit (7) = Cascade

Curvaceous /\ Joan? (3) = **Arc** (Joan of Arc)

Peter, icy, *say*, /causes\ **alarm** (5) = **Pan**ic (Peter Pan)

Put out of order /,\ called *in the* banker (7) = De**range**

Coloured /\ worker *in* transport (7) = Slan**ted**

JARGON

Every puzzle has its own unique flavour; a recognisable jargon of its own. These mental habits of the setters are a matter of their

Homograph (Jargon)

individual and recognisable styles. Some may, for example, refer homographically to a river as a flower or as a banker.
Put out of order /,\ <u>called</u> *in the* <u>banker</u> (7) = **De**range
European flower /with\ *utterly* <u>distinctive smell</u> (4) = Oder
<u>Nora</u> *Batty* /,\ **flower of Italy**? (4) = Arno
<u>I backed Ru</u> *wrongly* /producing\ a **bloomer** (9) = Rudbeckia

NUMERS
<u>51</u> <u>reprimanded</u> /were\ **released** (9) = **Li**berated
'Shake' /–\ <u>a great number</u> *included by* <u>a certain singer</u> (7)
    = Tremble

ABBREVIATIONS
Minute portion /of a\ ~~penny~~ <u>item</u> (8) = **P**article
Cake /for\ <u>member</u> *getting in the* <u>condiments</u> (7) = Cru**mp**et
Drinking-party /\ <u>song</u> *about* <u>America</u> (8) = Caro**usal**

MACARONI
~~Rugby,~~ *over* <u>an hour</u> /\ **in Germany** (4) = **R**uhr

Dash or hyphen

Sometimes a dash or hyphen is used as a fulcrum, but this happens rarely.

Power /–\ <u>mains at</u> *exchange* (7) = Stamina
Disappearing /–\ but not into thin air (10) = Dissolving
Delicate surgery /–\ *yet Dr isn't* *involved!* (9) = Dentistry
<u>Child</u> *has* <u>a</u> <u>pound</u> /–\ **the whole amount** (5) = Total
<u>Hat</u> *and* <u>pipe</u> *mislaid* /–\ **in the cemetery?** (7) = Epitaph
<u>Ordinary</u> <u>seaman</u> *first* /–\ **that's odd** (8) = **Ab**normal
<u>Football club</u> ~~lost~~ *twice* /–\ **will go down** (4) = Fall
<u>Spring,</u> *say,* <u>on Elba</u> *possibly* /–\ **how timely** (10) = Seasonable
<u>Work</u> *with* <u>Tim~~othy~~</u> *on* <u>one's</u> <u>twitch</u> /–\ **that's hopeful!** (10)
    = **Opti**mistic
Sign indicating <u>where road works usually are</u> /–\ **in front** (5)
    = Ahead

4. Nonconstruction Devices

Often the dash is part of a pasop and is used to mislead:

Spread ∧ ~~ruin~~ – ~~got~~ *about* ~~a pound~~ (9) = Marmalade
Rated ∧ ~~a page~~ – ~~commended~~ *for it* (9) = Appraised
~~Carol's~~ *after* ~~a single member~~ – ~~nothing~~ ∧ **special** (8) = Imposing
Awfully ~~decent – not~~ ∧ **relaxed though** (9) = Contented
~~Corset – an~~ *essential* /for\ **the older person** (8) = Ancestor
Indian nurse ∧ *from* ~~Bomb~~ay – a ~~hard worker~~ (4) = Ayah

Most of the time the hyphen is no more than an ordinary punctuation mark and may be ignored:

Given ~~to~~ *back*-~~street~~ ∧ **youngsters** (4) = Tots
Small crown ∧ *made from* ~~empty~~ ~~ice-cream container~~ (7) = Coronet
Slenderness /of\ ~~girl~~ *in* ~~the~~ *French* ~~ocean-going vessel~~ (8)
    = Leanness
After ~~half-time,~~ ~~I have~~ the ~~right~~ ∧ **fur** (7) = Miniver
Do well /with\ ~~professional~~ ~~representatives'~~ *back-up* (7) = Prosper
~~Student~~ ~~beat~~ ~~a~~ ∧ **pack-animal** (5) = Llama
~~Like a toss-up~~ /, it's\ **risky** (6) = Chancy
Theatre /-in-the-\ ~~round~~ (5) = Globe
Forms /of\ ~~take-over?~~ (8,6) = Adoption papers
~~House pet~~ /,\ **long-admired?** (4,9) = Firm favourite
~~Current~~ ~~set~~-*back* ∧ **may cause problems** (3,2) = Act up
Drinking-party ∧ ~~song~~ *about* ~~America~~ (8) = Carousal

Occasionally the same is true of the dash:

~~Daughter~~ – ~~one~~ of **23** (4) = Done
One who does may land in hot water – or cold (6,2,4,3)
    = Skates on thin ice
~~One who hits out~~ /– at a\ **blackleg?** (7) = Striker

Olapsek

> An olapsek is a crossword device that allows an **o**ver**lap** of the **s**ynonymcrux, **e**xposition and **k**eyword.

The overlapped part of the clue is between two fulcrum marks and should be included with the synonymcrux AND with the exposition : <u>Appreciate</u> something = Dig**it** = **something on foot**.
Some ~~nasty~~ <u>eye</u> = Stye = **eye infection**

<u>Appreciate</u> /\ **something** /\ **on foot** (5) = Dig**it**
Some ~~nasty~~ /\ **eye** /\ **infection** (4) = Stye
/\ **Composed** /\ <u>a</u> ~~little music~~ *medley* (4) = Calm
/\ **Ignore** /\ <u>being told you're sacked</u> (4,2,6) = Take no notice
In the /\ ~~main~~ **Castilians** /\ **viewed them as subjects** (5) = Incas
<u>Neat</u> /\ **barrier** /\ **on the way** (6-4) = Cattle-grid
<u>Remove</u> /\ **barriers** /\ **to prevent an attack?** (7) = **De**fence
<u>Runs for</u> /\ **100** /\ **years** (7) = Century
Some ~~other~~ /\ **measurement** /\ **unit** (5) = Therm
Something of an /\ ~~indentation~~ /\ (4) = Dent
/\ **Tear** Alec /\ *to pieces* (8) = Lacerate
<u>Tear</u> some /\ **rope** /\ **on the parachute** (3-4) = Rip-cord
There is prospect of /\ **success** /\ <u>in aerial battle</u> (7,2,3,3)
    = Victory in the air

Paraphrase

> To paraphrase is to express the meaning of a text in other words.

In the cryptic crossword clue paraphrasing is isolated so that the synonymcrux is paraphrased without regard for the rest of the clue. Equally, parts of the exposition are isolated for paraphrasing. It hardly ever happens that the whole clue is paraphrased as one unbroken sentence, except in the nosek (<u>no</u> <u>s</u>ynonymcrux, <u>e</u>xposition and <u>k</u>eyword). When the clue does have a synonymcrux the answer is always a paraphrase of it, as well as a special kind of paraphrase of the exposition.

Attract /\ <u>father</u> *bringing up* <u>ring</u> (6) = Ap**peal**
<u>Boy</u> *about* <u>to</u> *come up* /with\ **soup** (6) = **P**otage
Despot /has\ <u>car</u> *and rickety* <u>cart</u> (8) = **Auto**crat
<u>Girl</u> <u>able</u> *to recall* /a\ **whole lot of dates** (7) = **Alma**nac
<u>See</u> *differently first* <u>signal</u> /in\ **jargon** (12) = **Telegraph**ese
The scholar /takes\ <u>ages</u> *to* <u>sum</u> *up* (7) = **Eras**mus
<u>Voter</u> *turns tail with* <u>sort</u> /of\ **printing plate** (11) = **Electro**type

PART THREE

Types of Clue

There are essentially four broad categories of types of clue:
Construction types, in which the exposition yields up dixes that are used to construct the answer.
Deconstruction types, in which the exposition is taken apart to reveal the answer.
Reconstruction types, in which the exposition is taken apart to yield up dixes that are used to construct the answer.
Nonconstruction types, in which the answer is discovered, instead of constructed.

1. Construction-type Clues

Buildword

A buildword is a concatenation of lexical segments (linking parts of words together) derived from the clue and stacked in the answer in the manner indicated by the keywords. In the absence of keywords, stacking occurs from left to right. The lexical segments referred to are partwords, words, bitwords, parabrebits, abbreviations, initials, backwords, anagrams, dixes and dixemes.

An example (in a down clue)
Agreeing /with\ <u>many over boy worker</u> (9) = **Cons**on**a**nt
Agreeing /with\ <u>Hundred</u> on son ant
Agreeing /with\ C on son ant
Alternatively, with becomes co and many becomes n.
Agreeing /\ co <u>n~~umber~~</u> son ant

Buildword

Buildwords use a great diversity of devices:
Girl /has\ a large drink *as stated* (7) = Abigail (A big 'ail')
Homophone, splitword, parabrebit, stacking.

A buildword is essentially a 'stacking' clue. For examples see pages 56, 57, 62, 63, 65, 80 and 84.

Concon

The word concon is a **con**traction of **con**tainer and **con**tents. It describes a clue or device where one word is split in two to form a container for another word (the content) that is inserted into the split. Concons use whole words only.

Left ∧ a wild pig *in* its own fat (8) = Larboard (Boar in lard**)**
Obstinate person ∧ *has to put* energy *into* part (5) = Bi**go**t (Go in bit)
Object *to the inclusion of a* suit ∧ **inside the cover** (7) = En**case**d (Case in end)
List of explanations /from\ Gary *when admitting* defeat (8) = Gloss**ary** (Loss in Gary)
Fish /or\ cut grass *round* hotel (6) = Min**n**ow (Inn in mow)
Man *accepting* alternative ∧ **spirit** (6) = Morale
Salesman *in the* money ∧ **to settle in advance** (6) = Pre**pay**
Hurried *around with a* lubricant /, but\ **it didn't improve things!** (7) = Spoiled (sped around oil)
Speculation /that\ the right man *will go in* (6) = Theory
Try *to include* an undergarment /in\ **the disguise** (8) = Travesty
Small stream *in* part of India /where there was\ **a large ape** (7) = Gorilla

2. Deconstruction-type Clues

Undix

> An undix is a type of clue (or device) in which a dix is removed from a word or a tword to leave a baseword or bitwords suitable for constructing an answer, or to be used to construct the answer itself.

A **dixeme** is the minimal constructive unit of words in word games and the central concern of dixology. A **dix** is the constructive unit of which words are built in word games, though not necessarily the smallest possible unit.

The word dix is taken from 'appendix' and literally means, 'That which may be appended (addixed) or removed (undixed) like an appendix.' However, dix must be distinguished from appendix because a dix is a piece of a word taken from a word to be used to make a new word. The unit that is removed (undixed) has no regular form or length. It has no meaning. It may, by coincidence, be an abbreviation of the word. It may be a syllable, a partword, a digraph, a morpheme or an affix too, but the coincidence is to be ignored. The new word may be a partword of the original word, or it may be a wholly new construction.

She ∧ gets *the same bit of* l̲u̲ck *twice* (4) = Lu**lu**

Beheadment

> A beheadment removes the head (or first part) of a word and discards it, while the remainder is still a word.

Doesn't begin to get g̶e̶ared to ∧ **having sound detectors** (5) = Eared

Frequently /is\ m̲o̲r̲e̲ ̲m̲a̲l̲l̲e̲a̲b̲l̲e̲, *removing top* (5) = Often (s̲o̲f̲t̲e̲n̲)

Curtailment

> A curtailment removes the tail (or last part) of a word and discards it.

<u>Heather</u> *dropping* a̶ ∧ **boy** (4) = Eric (<u>Eric</u>a̶)
<u>Girl</u> *without* a̶ ∧ **messenger** (5) = Angel (<u>Angel</u>a̶)

Disheartenment

> A disheartenment removes the heart (or centre) of a word and discards it.

Being stupid /,\ *I leave* <u>Den</u>i̶s̶e̶ (8) = Dense (<u>Den</u>i̶s̶e̶)
N̶o̶t̶h̶i̶n̶g̶ *less than* a <u>lifeless</u> ∧ **deity** (5) = Woden (<u>wo</u>o̶d̶en)

Two disheartenments used as a device in a buildword:

Ch̶a̶r̶l̶e̶s̶ t̶h̶e̶ h*eartless* /was\ **sexually virtuous** (6) Chaste (<u>Ch</u>a̶r̶l̶e̶s̶)
   (t̶h̶e̶)

3. Reconstruction-type Clues

Acronym

> An acronym is a word or name made of the stacked initials of a phrase or series of words.

Acronyms are rare in crosswords. Too rare, since they are a delight to find:

Indian worker /\ *starts to* d~~ream happily of bigger income~~ (5)
= Dhobi
/\ **C~~ompose~~d** /\ a ~~little~~ m~~usic~~ *medley* (4) = Calm

The keyword *initially* does not always indicate an acronym:

Atrocious crime /in\ house in Y~~ork~~ *initially* (8) = Villainy

Anagram

> An anagram is a word or phrase made by transposition of letters of another word or phrase.

When setting a crossword it is difficult to find a one-word anagram for the letters available in an answer. It is easy to make words that use some of the letters of the answer. Most anagrams are transcribed into more than one word because compilation is easier. One of these words is sometimes a cumbersome word because once the first word has been made the remaining letters cannot be used well or cleverly. These awkward words include names and contractions. The contractions are glaringly obvious because of the apostrophe they contain. Sometimes the odd letters are used as initials or an abbreviation. One or two letters may even be put into a whole new word, to be extracted later as a partbit. Many anagrams are revealed by their forced phraseology. When their obviously stilted style is combined with a name or apostrophe of possession or elision, an anagram is certain to be present.

SOURCES OF LETTERS FOR ANAGRAMS

ONE WORD
Crush /\ <u>repulsive</u> *concoction* (9) = Pulverise
<u>Intrude</u> *clumsily* /,\ **lacking experience** (7) = Untried

MULTIPLE WORD ANAGRAMS
<u>Stale tuna</u> *removed* /from\ **the territory** (9) = Sultanate
Notorious /\ <u>gorge I use</u> *by arrangement* (9) = Egregious
Changes <u>in it are</u> /due to\ **inactivity** (7) = Inertia
<u>Can veto</u> *conversion* /into\ **foreign currency** (7) = Centavo
Acrobatic display /\ <u>last mouser</u> *could have given* (10) = Somersault

INITIALS AND ABBREVIATIONS
Crooked <u>NCO's</u> /\ **swindles** (4) = Cons
Torn skin /of\ *unfortunate* <u>GI Alan</u> (6) = Agnail

ODD LETTER ELSEWHERE (TRANSINSERTIONS)
At the ~~wee~~k<u>end</u> <u>a chair</u> *is put out* /\ **in Pakistan** (7) = Karachi
Madly <u>thirsting</u>, *when it's* h~~et~~ *inside*, /to have\ **something on in bed** (10) = Nightshirt
Fancy <u>sweet</u> ~~had~~ *shortly* /been\ **cooked slowly**! (6) = Stewed
D~~octo~~<u>r</u> *contains inordinate* <u>greed</u> /making\ **the boat** (7) = Dredger

INDICATORS OF ANAGRAMS

NAMES
<u>Lie Nora</u> *concocted about* /\ **wing-tip** (7) = Aileron
Torn skin /of\ *unfortunate* <u>GI Alan</u> (6) = Agnail
Things worth remembering /\ <u>I blame Mario</u> *about* (11) = Memorabilia
Great /\ <u>Elgar</u> *composition* (5) = Large

Anagram (Indicators of anagrams)

STILTED STYLE
Stilted style includes the use of peculiar words and strained syntax.

Lie Nora *concocted* /*about*\ **wing-tip** (7) = Aileron
Torn skin /of\ *unfortunate* GI Alan (6) = Agnail
Acrobatic display /\ last mouser *could have given* (10) = Somersault
Notorious /\ gorge I use *by arrangement* (9) = Egregious
University trainin' a *new* /\ **believer** (9) = Unitarian

ELLIPSIS
Ellipsis is the omission from a sentence of words needed to complete construction or sense. Missing articles or prepositions are useful indicators of anagrams. (Their conspicuous presence is often indicative of the need for stacking bitwords in a buildword.) Very often words normally used in ordinary sentence construction need to be omitted, lest they impede an anagram by becoming part of the exposition.

University trainin' a *new* /\ **believer** (9) = Unitarian

The verb is incomplete to the extent that it does not even indicate tense (… is, was or will be training?). This example is really a buildword that uses an anagram as a device, and 'a' conspicuously indicates the need for stacking.

Can veto *conversion* /into\ **foreign currency** (7) = Centavo

The clue lacks a subject that would be present in normal sentence construction. The subject would do nothing but impede the anagram, so it has been omitted.

APOSTROPHE OF ELISION
Separate /\ act he'd *developed* (6) = Detach
Ben's no fraternal *kind* /\ **that cannot be passed on** (3-12)
    = Non-transferable
Rene's *upset* /by\ **expression of contempt** (5) = Sneer
University trainin' a *new* /\ **believer** (9) = Unitarian

Elision may be required en route to the answer:

Fancy <u>sweet</u> ~~had~~ *shortly* /been\ **cooked slowly**! (6) = Stewed

APOSTROPHE OF POSSESSION
Crooked <u>NCO's</u> ∧ **swindles** (4) = Cons
<u>Then city's</u> *production* /is\ **artificially produced** (9) = Synthetic

An apostrophe of possession may be required in the answer:

Is content with present achievements /,\ <u>reason nurse let loss</u>
   deteriorate (5,2,4,7) = Rests on one's laurels

COGNATE ANAGRAMS
A cognate anagram is one of an anagram pair of related meaning:

<u>Propose</u> *motion?* ∧ **He would do the converse** (7) = Opposer
Instruments of war /from\ <u>Mars</u> (4) = Arms
Mars, the god of war, yields two cognate anagrams: Arms and Rams.

Sometimes an anagram depends on the clue for the context that
makes it cognate:

Tolerant philosophy ∧ *confounded* <u>all evident evil</u> (4,3,3,4)
   = Live and let live
Lake ∧ *formed when* <u>river rose</u> *dangerously* (9) = Reservoir
This old timer ∧ *won't run* in <u>dry places</u> (9) = Clepsydra

COHERENT ANAGRAMS

> Coherent anagrams are adjacent anagrams used with coherent
> sense within a phrase or sentence. For example, palest pastel,
> cheap peach, one's nose. They differ from cognate anagrams
> because they have no related meaning to each other.

Coherent anagrams function as keywords in clues. On
examination of the clue it does not take long to recognise the

presence of an anagram, but one may not realise that a third anagram is required as answer. Fortunately crossletters soon remedy the oversight.

Shops /for\ <u>smart</u> <u>trams</u> (5) = Marts
<u>Pirates</u> <u>traipse</u> /to\ **meetings** (7) = Parties
<u>Priests</u> <u>persist</u> /in finding\ **fairies** (7) = Sprites
<u>Ransom</u> <u>Romans</u> /for\ **farms** (6) = Manors
The <u>dame</u> <u>made</u> /\ **cheese** (4) = Edam
The <u>dame</u> *made* /\ **cheese** (4) = Edam
<u>Tersest</u> **testers** (7) = Setters
Fighters /\ <u>wrestle</u> and <u>swelter</u> (7) = Welters
<u>Writhe</u>, <u>wither</u> /and become\ **paler** (5) = Whiter

Coherent anagrams do not always yield an anagram for an answer:

What made <u>the girl</u> <u>lighter</u>? (7) = Anagram

KEYWORDS
The keywords used in anagrams are often distinctly cognate.

<u>Men test-drive a</u> *convertible* /to get\ **publicity** (13) = Advertisement
<u>Then city's</u> *production* /is\ **artificially produced** (9) = Synthetic
<u>Can veto</u> *conversion* /into\ **foreign currency** (7) = Centavo
~~Doctor~~ *contains inordinate* <u>greed</u> /making\ **the boat** (7) = Dredger

'Convertible' and 'inordinate' are remarkably clever cognate keywords and are probably the product of sheer genius. Both words are very fixed in their meaning by their conventional use, which is achieved here by having both perfectly in context. It requires a deliberate and very skilful misreading of the text to see the meaning of the keyword. Only by misreading does 'convertible' mean the conversion of letter order. The meaning of the word is pushed to its limit when 'inordinate' means not inordinate, i.e., not 1st, 2nd, 3rd. The metaphoric use of 'inordinate' has overshadowed and replaced the original, literal meaning.

Hidden words

> A hidden word is found inside other words. Hidden word types include partwords, backwords, splitwords, bridgewords, reversals (and beheadments, curtailments, disheartenments).

Hiden words are no longer a type of clue but have become a collective form for several clue types.

Partwords

> A partword is a word that is wholly contained by another word.

Favourite /\ *in the* ~~com~~pet~~ition~~ (3) = Pet
Crew /\ *from a* ~~fr~~eight~~er~~ (5) = Eight

Backword

> A backword is a word that can be reversed to make a new and different word. Backwords differ from palindromes, which are words or phrases that remain unchanged when spelled backwards.

BACKWORDS IN THE CLUE
Backwords can be used as a specie of hidden word so that the answer is plain to see in the clue.

Badly made /\ **cheese** (4) = Edam
Vile sin /is\ live *regression* (4) = Evil

BACKWORDS IN THE ANSWER
Since the clue usually defines the answer twice it makes much sense to use backwords as answers. The answer is defined once in the synonymcrux and once again by its backword having a synonym in the exposition. In this way the backword is seen only in the answer. These examples are all down clues.

Stake /for\ <u>mountain</u> *climbing* (4) = Ante (Etna)
Saw /\ <u>music</u> *upside-down* (5) = Tenon (Nonet)
Space /\ <u>to tie up</u> (4) = Room (Moor)
<u>Have fun</u> *up* /in\ the **bar** (5) = Lever (Revel)

KEYWORDS
The keywords indicating backwords are direction sensitive. 'Up', 'climbing' and 'upside-down' are found in down clues. 'Back' and 'returning' are found in across clues. 'About', 'retiring' and 'reverse' are found in down and across clues.

SHORT BACKWORDS
More than 80 per cent of backwords are three, four or five letters long. Few backwords are longer than five letters. This is because of the way some letters are commonly found together, but seldom in reverse order. Longer words very quickly contain one of these irreversible combinations (ing, ck, ch, sh, com, rse, etc) and this fact renders them irreversible in toto. When long words form backwords it is often because they were deliberately designed to be backwords (e.g., Onalosi and Isolano) and their meanings will be antonymic. Even long palindromes are based on short words

Able was I ere I saw Elba
A man, a plan, a canal: Panama!
Are we not drawn onward, we few, drawn onward to new era?

Incidentally, one sees how splitwords are used to create palindromes:

!amanaP :lanac a nalp a nam A
?are wen ot drawno nward ,wef ew ,drawno nward ton ew erA

COGNATE BACKWORDS
A cognate backword is one of a backword pair of related meaning:

<u>Hits</u> *back* /in\ **fight** (4) = Spar (Raps)
<u>Hit</u> *back* /with\ a **whip** (4) = Taws (Swat)

COHERENT BACKWORDS

Coherent backwords are adjacent backwords used with coherent sense within a phrase or sentence. They are used to make long palindromes (Able was I ere I saw Elba. Are we not drawn onward, we few, drawn onward to new era?) They do not often appear in crossword clues.

Reversal

A reversal is the creation of a word from a series of letters which is read backwards. Both partwords and bridgewords occur as reversals in clues. These are not backword clues, because the true backword is a whole word that has its own meaning when read in either direction.

PARTWORDS

Name /\ *backwards in* ~~alphabetical order~~ (4) = Cite
Bird /\ *on* ~~iceberg~~ *suffering a bit of a setback* (5) = Grebe

BRIDGEWORDS

In backing ~~army CO I displayed~~ /\ **stupidity** (6) = Idiocy
Frequently /\ *arises in* ~~argument, fortunately~~ (3) = Oft

Splitword

Splitwords are formed by regrouping (splitting) a series of letters. Odds on, odd son. This specific duality of meaning is central to the ambiguity of this type of clue.

SPLITWORDS IN THE ANSWER

<u>Kill mother</u> /for\ **some land** (6) = do**ma**in (Do ma in)
<u>Champion debtor</u> /,\ **one who confers gifts** (8) = **Best**ower
<u>Out more often</u> /and\ **sleeping rough** (8) = Home**less**
I <u>speak maliciously</u> /about\ the **inhabitant** (8) = I**s**lander
<u>Incompetent</u> /\ **worthy** (7) = No**table**
Cleaner /\ <u>to put</u> a <u>man off</u> (9) = Deter**gent**
He has been instructed to vote /\ <u>for two unknowns</u> (5) = **Pro**xy
    (Pro x & y)
<u>Advances</u> /\ **a member of the family** (7) = Step**son**

Dispute *after* dispute /for\ the **winger** (7) = Spar**row**
Eccentric boy? ∧ **Sure thing!** (4,2) = Odd**s on**

SPLITWORDS IN THE CLUE
*Alast*air in three words /produces\ **a final work** (4-4) = Swan-
song (A last air)

A word is often split between a keyword and the exposition.

Spanish nobleman ∧ concealed gaol*break* (7) = Hidalgo
(gaol *break*)
At the ~~week~~*end* a chair *is put out* ∧ **in Pakistan** (7) = Karachi
(week end)
T*in* spoon ∧ **precisely** (4,2) = Spot on ('T' in spoon)

In a variation on the theme, a buildword is created by discovering
a hidden word in a rare clue that ignores every second (or odd)
letter:

Eight ∧ ~~botch theft~~ *after ignoring the odds* (5) = Octet

Bridgeword

> A bridgeword is a hidden word formed by the last part of the
> first word and the first part of the last word of consecutive
> words.

Bridgewords are among the easiest of clues to solve once one is
aware of their existence. Unless one recognises the presence of
the bridgeword in a clue it really makes no sense at all, especially
if one is unfamiliar with the concept of the synonymcrux. If
considered as normal questions and answers these examples
constitute sheer nonsense. The untrained eye does not see the
hidden bridgeword.

A **stake** ∧ *in a* ~~buoy~~ant ~~economy~~ (4) = Ante
~~The leng~~thy *part* /for\ **a lady** (5) = Helen
Some ~~fi~~ne ed~~wardian silver~~ /is\ **essential** (4) = Need

Bridgeword

Of all clues it is probably the bridgeword that most uniformly adheres to the ideal construction of the cryptic clue. Bridgewords almost always have a distinct synonymcrux, exposition and keyword, and often a word fulcrum.

Go too far /from\ ~~d~~over do~~wnhill~~ (6) = Overdo
Some ~~existing edifice~~ /was\ **slightly coloured** (6) = Tinged
~~Octo~~ber ~~lingers~~ *in* /\ **the city** (6) = Berlin
Among ~~th~~em an~~other~~ /\ **virile fellow** (2-3) = He-man
~~The cho~~r~~eographer~~ *covered* /\ the **sound reflection** (4) = Echo
Partly ~~f~~lat-~~chested~~? /There's\ **a catch** (5) = Latch
~~Disr~~obes ~~eventually~~ *holding in* /\ **fat** (5) = Obese

There is always an exception:

One *of the* ~~best~~ ar~~tistes~~ (4) = Star
No clear synonymcrux, exposition, keyword or fulcrum, since they overlap.

The bridgeword may include a partword and so span three words:

Some ~~drag~~oons laugh, ~~taking~~ fierce attack = Onslaught

The most common reason for using an apostrophe in clues is that the letters adjacent to it are needed to construct the answer:

In the ~~kindergar~~ten 'e men~~tioned~~ the /\ **flat** (8) = Tenement

Interclue

An interclue is a clue that requires the answer of another clue (the referent clue) to be inserted into itself, in the place where it refers to 'another clue'.

The interclue is mechanically simple, and not very exciting intellectually. More often than not it is nothing more than an irritation because it is easily solved once the referent clue is solved. The irritation arises from the need to solve the two clues in a specific order. No other kind of clue requires the prior solution of another clue, no matter how helpful crossletters may be. The usual method for solving interclues is as follows.

1. Determine which clue is being referred to.
2. Solve the referent clue.
3. Return to the interclue and remove the referring clue number from the body of the clue.
4. Substitute the answer of the referent clue for the removed clue number.
5. Solve as usual.

NORMAL INTERCLUES

9d) Men test-drive a *convertible* /to get\ **publicity** (13)
    = ADVERTISEMENT
Men *into* 9? **Correct!** (5) = Amend
Men *into* AD~~VERTISEMENT~~? **Correct!** (5) = Amend

18d) **Downfall** /of\ one *in a* hurry (4) = RUIN
Wiping out 18 down (11) = Destruction
Wiping out /\ **RUIN** (11) = Destruction

11a) **Stay** /\ second (7) = SUPPORT
Bible gets 11 across here in church (7) = Lectern
Bible gets SUPPORT here in church (7) = Lectern

11a) **A record** some youngsters ~~cannot endure~~ (4) = NOTE
Change 11, though sound (4) = Tone
Change NOTE, /though\ **sound** (4) = Tone

24d) **Stupid person** /,\ one *with* Dorothy *going round* island (5)
   = IDIOT
A 24 comes back for a brush (5) = Loofa
A IDIOT *comes back* /for\ a **brush** (5) = Loofa
Paraphrase:
A FOOL *comes back* /for\ a **brush** (5) = Loofa
This puzzle has no 24 across clue, which is why 'down' is omitted, unlike the next example.

24a) A tax popular with racegoers! (5) = ASCOT
Hurry *alongside* track such as /\ **24 across** (10) = Racecourse
Hurry *alongside* track such as /\ **ASCOT** (10) = Racecourse

MUTUAL INTERCLUES

When both clues refer to each other they undermine the rule that one clue cannot be solved unless the other has first been solved. In this case neither can be solved unless the other is solved first!

28a) **8** /\ *composed by heartless* ~~rogue~~ to bind (6) = RECORD
8d) Compose love lines /for\ **28** (9) = INVENTORY (invent o ry)
Invent o ~~railway~~ /for\ **RECORD** (9) = Inventory
INVENTORY /\ *composed by heartless* ~~rogue~~ to bind (6) = Record

The game becomes very interesting. The mutual reference indicates that the two answers are synonyms of each other. By an extension of this logic the two expositions should contain the same meaning. Herein lies the key to solving the clues: join the two expositions together as though they were a single clue that has no synonymcrux. With consideration of the num and crossletters, solve first the one then the other exposition. Verify the answer by substitution.

Interclues sometimes do not require substitution. The mutual interclue establishes the rule is that the answer of the interclue is a synonym of the referent clue's answer (because the latter functions as the synonymcrux of the interclue). In consequence of the establishment of this principle it is no longer necessary to substitute the referent answer into the interclue.

23d) **Tired** /of\ <u>everything trendy</u> (3,2) = ALL IN
<s>Daughter</s> – <u>one</u> of **23** (4) = Done
<s>Daughter</s> – <u>one</u> /of\ **ALL IN** (4) = Done

The interclue may be solved by finding a synonym for the referent clue's answer.

ODD INTERCLUES
On occasion the referent answer does not function perfectly as a synonymcrux. As with the mutual interclue this example must be solved by using two expositions.

10d) <u>Passage</u> *to* <u>Scottish island</u> <s>learner</s> took was **temporary** (12)
  = TRANSITIONAL
Startin' badly *in* <u>10 down</u> (7) = Transit
<u>Startin'</u> *badly* /\ *in* <u>TRANSIT<s>IONAL</s></u> (7) = Transit (an anagram and a partword)

Occasionally the answer for one clue is spread over two lights. The second light has no clue, only a reference to the first clue. This is not uncommon when the answer is a phrase.

Down
2d and 20a) <u>Proprietary medicament which too few buy</u> (4,2,3,6)
  = Drug in the market
Across
20a) See 2 down (6) = Market

The grid for this puzzle reveals that the light at 2 down has only nine squares. 20 across has six squares. Between the two the whole phrase fits. Most often these phrases occupy adjacent or serial lights and are simply noted as:

Across
4 and 5) Xxxx xxxx x xxxx xxxxxxx (n,n,n,n)

There is no referring interclue, since it is obvious that the answer runs across two lights.

Palindrome

> A palindrome is a word or phrase that reads the same backwards as forwards.

Either way /it's\ **out of the question** (3,2) = Not on
Time /to\ *return unchanged* (4) = Noon
More ruddy ∧ *toing and froing*! (6) = Redder
Either way /it's\ **an exclamation of surprise** (3) = Aha
Quick look ∧ *both ways* (4) = Peep

Partbits

> A partbit is the opposite of beheadments, curtailments and disheartenments. In these three instances a letter or dix is deleted and the bulk of the word which remains is used in the answer. But in the case of the partbit the bulk of the word is discarded and only a letter or a dix is used in building a new word. Partbits are a collective name for four types of clue: addix, condix, transdeletion and transinsertion.

Addix

> An addix describes a previously undixed dix used to construct an answer. In the addix the extracted dix is not discarded to leave a partword but is used itself in the construction of the answer. The dix in question is always first undixed from the source word and then addixed into the target word, the answer.

Leading ~~seaman~~, <u>given short notice</u> /, was\ **unhappy** (3)
   = Sad (~~seaman~~)
<u>Hurried</u> *with* ~~Dutch~~ *leader's* /\ **currency** (4) = Rand (~~Dutch~~)
~~Could~~ *start with* <u>fruit</u> /and\ **a morsel of fried food** (4) = Chip
Banded appearance of rocks /caused by\ <u>early</u> *movement* in
   ~~Greek~~ *capital* (8) = Layering
Flower /\ *might* <u>open</u> *before end of* ~~May~~ (5) = Peony
Ward off /\ <u>Catherine</u> *before end of* ~~day~~ (5) = Parry

Addixes may be regular abbreviations, in which case they do not
have keywords.

<u>Pro</u>~~fessional~~ <u>examination</u> /giving rise to\ **complaint** (7) = Pro**test**
From <u>north-east</u>, ~~Augustus~~ *brought* /\ **hot wine** (5) = Negus
Agenda /for\ <u>ed</u>~~ucation~~ *in* <u>German school</u> (8) = Sched**ule**

SYNONYM AND DIX
The synonym and the dix used to construct the answer have their
origin in the exposition; the synonymcrux is always a synonym of
the answer.

<u>Do not stand</u> a ~~Revolutionary~~ *leader* /taking\ the **instrument** (5)
   = Sitar
<u>Open land</u> *at both ends of* <u>L</u>angle<u>y</u> /,\ **generally** (8) = Commonly
(Both dixemes were indicated by the keywords.)
One follows /\ <u>smash-hit</u> *with* <u>o</u>~~perational-research~~ (9) = Success**or**
(Both dixemes are abbreviations and initials.)
<u>Said</u> *before second half of* ~~July~~ /\ **in the appointed manner** (8)
   = Stated**ly**
Clearly /but\ <u>lazily</u> *having most of the* <u>luc</u>~~k~~ *first* (7) = Lucidly

The dix that is used in the answer may be extracted from the
synonym (sack):

Pouch /makes up\ *most of the* <u>large bag</u> (3) = Sac

BITWORD AND DIX
When a partword is removed from a tword a dix remains. It may be used to construct an answer.

He really *lost his friend* /\ **at this place** (4) = He**re** (**ally** was removed from really)

The keyword is indicative of the extraction of the partword. The remaining bitword (He) and dix (re) must be stacked from left to right in the absence of instruction to the contrary.

To indicate a bridgeword the clue must be rephrased.

He really remained in /\ **this place** (4) = He**re**

DIX AND DIX
She /\ gets the same bit of luck *twice* (4) = Lu**lu**

Condix

> A condix is a container and contents word where either the container or the content (or both) is a dix instead of a word. (A concon is a word that contains another word, eg: Rag + tin = ra**tin**g).

Lingering behind /\ a horse left *in line* (10) = Stra**gg**ling (String containing a gg and l)

String is obviously split to form a container word, but there is no contents word. Thus no concon. *A, gg* and *l* are dixemes addixed (i.e. a dix added) into the container word. A fine example of how the principle of one type of clue (concon) is applied in another type of clue (buildword). It is merely the principle that is applied. From out of the concon thus grew the condix.

Poet /\ writes note *held by disheartened* singer (7) = **S**penser

Both dixes remain once a central dix is removed from singer. This is not a simple one step disheartenment that leaves the answer standing in the form of a partword. The addix is required to construct the answer. Thus we see that the addix is a two step construction (Undix, then addix) as all the earlier examples show. One, remove dix from clue. Two, put dix in answer.

I <u>draw</u> *most of the* <u>post</u> *outside* /,\ it's **a condition of agreement** (11) = Sti**pul**ation
Here the inserted dix uses a curtailment of pull, but without extracting a partword.

Bore /is\ *shockingly* <u>rude</u> *in the* <u>end</u> (7) = En**dur**ed
The dixemes of <u>rude</u> contained by the word <u>end</u>.

Crazy /\ <u>plan</u> <u>aide</u> *entertained* (6) = Mad**c**ap
The dixemes of the abbreviation <u>adc</u> in the word <u>map</u>.

Arranged <u>search</u>, *about* <u>four</u>/, for\ **old records** (8) = Arch**ive**s
It would seem that the clue is an anagram that incorporates an addix. But the keywords too strongly suggest a container and contents, especially since the fulcrum perfectly clearly isolates the synonymcrux. This is a condix that uses anagram as a device. Both the container and the contents are dixes, not words.

Transdeletion

> In the transdeletion the answer is an anagram of the remaining letters once a dixeme (an odd single letter) has been deleted, for example: Instant, taints, saint, tins, nit, in, I.

No recor~~d~~ *endlessly arranged* /for\ the **singer** (7) = Crooner

Transinsertion

In the transinsertion the answer is an anagram of the total letters once a dixeme (an odd single letter) has been added. For example, I, in, nit, tins, saint, taints, instant.

Madly thirsting, *when it's* h~~e~~t *inside*, /to have\ **something on in bed** (10) = Nightshirt
Fancy sweet ~~had~~ *shortly* /been\ **cooked slowly**! (6) = Stewed

There are always exceptions, which are really variations on a theme.

At the ~~wee~~k*end* a chair *is put out* /\ **in Pakistan** (7) = Karachi
D~~octo~~r *contains inordinate* greed /making\ **the boat** (7) = Dredger

4. Nonconstruction-type Clues

Ammel

An ammel is a crossword clue where the headword of a lemma (or dictionary entry) is the answer and its definition is the clue. Ammels include synonymclues (Bog-myrtle (4) = gale) and genus-and-specie clues (Tree (5) = maple). Ammel is a backword of lemma because one needs to use a dictionary backwards to solve the clue.

THE ABSENT FULCRUM
In the ammel the clue often has no fulcrum because the exposition includes the synonymcrux.

Organ stop with string tone (5) = Gamba
Sings without knowing the words (4) = Hums
Following one after another (2,10) = In succession
Substitutes for missing members (10,5) = Artificial limbs

In the last example 'for' is not the fulcrum because missing members in no way redefines substitutes. The concept of 'X for Y' cannot apply.

An unusual example:
And and or or or or and (5) = Andor
Andor is the same as and/or, but without the /. Either way, it is pronounced the same. Andor means one of two things: either 'and' as well as 'or'; or alternatively, 'or' instead of 'and'. Thus it means (And and or) or (or or and). Remove the brackets to get 'and and or or or or and'.

AMMEL IN EXPOSITION

An ammel is also a crossword device where an ammel is the exposition or part of the exposition (as is the case with most extended synonymtwins).

<u>Television cabinet</u> *designed* /for\ **comfort** (7) = Console
<u>With no idea</u> /being\ **uncaring** (11) = Thoughtless

AMMEL IN SYNONYMCRUX

Ammels are frequently found where the synonymcrux is made of many words.

<u>Trip</u> <u>over</u> /and\ **come upon something unexpectedly** (7,6)
= Stumble across
Containing the most subject-matter /but\ <u>of least interest to a</u>
   <u>vegetarian</u> (8) = Meatiest

NO KEYWORDS

There are no keywords that indicate ammels, but ammels are easily identified by the coherence of phrases and their definitive formulation.

In succession means 'following one after another'.
Artificial limbs are 'substitutes for missing members'.
A console is a 'television cabinet'.

Antonym

> An antonym is a word of contrary meaning to another, e.g., high and low. It is the opposite of a synonym. The word antonym is also used to mean a type of crossword clue where antonyms are the basis of the exposition, and used to determine the answer.

THE NEGATIVE KEYWORD
Usually the synonymcrux retains its usual place and function, but the exposition is so formulated that it would negate the meaning of the synonymcrux but for the presence of a negative keyword.

Didn't make a connection /when it\ **melted** (5) = Fused
Take away something /that\ *isn't* concrete (8) = Abstract
Stupid /,\ *unlike* crossword solvers (8) = Clueless
Rejection /*despite*\ lady's commendation (11) = Disapproval

The answer of this last example cleverly uses a splitword that negates itself (Di's approval).

AN ANTONYMCRUX?
Antonyms can be constructed in such a way that there is no synonymcrux and the exposition becomes an antonymcrux. The keyword indicates the need for a reversal of meaning.

Easily *converse* (6) = Hardly
Running /\ *the wrong way* (11) = Mismanaging

Classical allusion

> The classical allusion clue refers to a famous literary work or a character therein or its author.

Doubly evil /\ **sailor** (6) = Sinbad
No man's land taken over by Napoleon (6,4) = Animal Farm
Amy, for one /, is\ **a tramp** (5) = March

Classical allusion

'Man is by nature a political . . .' (Aristotle) (6) = Animal
'And Thou beside me singing . . .' (Omar Khayyam) (2,3,10)
    = In the wilderness

Debono

The Debono is a type of clue that is named to honour Edward De Bono because its solution requires no more than a bit of lateral thinking. Often these clues seem to be puns, but there are many of them that involve no pun at all.

STRUCTURE
The Debono uses none of the devices of cryptic clues. It lacks the ideal structure of the cryptic clue. These examples have no synonymcruxes, keywords or fulcrums. The entire clue is an exposition that manages to define the answer twice

In orbit, one looks out (7) = Eyeball
Stern guide (6) = Rudder
Curvaceous Joan? (3) = Arc
Dotty type (7) = Braille
Period, of course, without ups and downs (4,6) = Flat season
    (It depends on how one reads it: A time, of (or pertaining to)
    the racecourse, when there are no jump races.)

MISDIRECTION
As is the case with most lateral thinking problems, there is a strong element of misdirection in the Debono.

Highland fling (7,3,5) = Tossing the caber
Curvaceous Joan? (3) = Arc
Flat-finding agencies (6,6) = Spirit levels
One taking stock of others (7) = Rustler
In orbit, one looks out (7) = Eyeball

'One' is usually a keyword that indicates a humer, and in the last example 'it' is eschewed to misdirect.

General knowledge

General knowledge is a wide and non-specialised knowledge. As applied in any way to crosswords it is a misnomer, because crosswords require a very wide, specialised and in-depth knowledge of all subjects. Yet it aptly names a specific specie of clue; the clue whose answer cannot be found other than by knowing (or guessing, and then confirming).

STRUCTURE
The best of these clues conform partially in structure and are twice defined with a regular synonymcrux. There are no keywords in general knowledge clues.

First post /\ **lady** (5) = Penny
Jenny /\ **the architect** (4) = Wren (Sir Christopher Wren)
Jenny /\ who went to sea (4) = Wren
    (A wren was a member of the Women's Royal Naval Service)
Vacuum /left by\ former FBI chief (6) = Hoover
Amy, for one, /is a\ **tramp** (5) = March
    (Amy March from *Little Women* by Louisa May Alcott)
Darling /\ dog responsible for guarding children (4) = Nana
    (Peter Pan)

The chief pleasure of these clues lies not in finding the answer, but in discovering the link between the two definitions of the clue. Unfortunately some of these clues are much less sophisticated and lack an exposition and fulcrum. Clues like this do not belong in the cryptic crossword because they are straight ammels:

Aviation spirit (7) = Gremlin
    (RAF slang, apparently popularised by Roald Dahl when he was a RAF pilot and war correspondent. The publication of the word in wartime newspapers meant that it was instantly spread throughout the RAF and adopted by all its members in everyday use. Gremlins were described by him as invisible beings on planes who were responsible for unexplained mechanical failures.)

General knowledge

CONTEXT

The puzzle in which one finds a clue may have been written for a specific market or publication, often one with a specialised readership. *The Actuary* is such a magazine and it has a regular crossword of its own. At the time of the centenary of the institute of actuaries there appeared a clue whose answer depended on knowing about the centenary, as every actuary did. However, the syndication of newspapers and the shrinking of the global village have had the consequence that puzzles may be resold andor exported to foreign media. One assumes that Cannon and Ball are a team of British comedians, known locally but not internationally. They appear, by way of a homophone, in a South African newspaper magazine whose puzzle was imported from the UK

Pair of comedians might fire this? (10) = Cannonball

From the same foreign magazine one gets these examples.

Period, of course, without ups and downs (4,6) = Flat season
South Africa has no jump races, hence no flat season.

The main road /from\ home counties, abroad (6) = **Se**away
South Africans have no counties, nor any knowledge of home counties.

Horse-race in the Midlands? (5) = Derby
The Derby or the Midlands mean little outside of Britain.

Scottish Cape ∧ **Town** (9) = Inverness
Scottish ∧ **Cape Town**? A very misleading clue when exported to Cape Town from Britain!

Here are some random examples indicating cultural context.

John of Orange? (4) = Peel
Odd ∧ street to be in when in debt (5) = Queer
Penny ~~used to buy this~~ ∧ **pipe** (7) = Whistle

Murder victim ∧ <u>pronounced fit!</u> (4) = Able
  (Easy for Christian cultural groups)
<u>Currently</u> <u>the chief</u> ∧ **form of jazz?** (10) = Mainstream
Vacuum /left by\ **former FBI chief** (6) = Hoover
<u>Disintegrating</u> ∧ **old borough** (6) = Rotten

Homophone

> A homophone is a word that is pronounced like another, but with a different spelling and meaning.

KEYWORDS
Homophones have easy keywords that stick out like sore thumbs.

Tense ∧ <u>whilst being given instructions,</u> *we hear* (4) = Taut
Fill cracks with filler /or\ <u>stopper,</u> *we hear* (5) = Caulk
A number ∧ <u>had a meal,</u> *we hear* (5) = Eight
<u>Rugby player</u> *we hear* ∧ **smoking pipe** (6) = Hookah
<u>Two pairs</u> *heard* /to be\ **exquisite** (3-3) = Too-too
Sounds <u>a good player</u> /– \ **give up!** (4) = Cede
Sounds like <u>a man</u> /of\ **letters** (4) = Mail
Sounds like <u>a bit of</u> ∧ **tranquillity** (5) = Peace
<u>Confident</u>-*sounding* ∧ **dramatist** (4) = Shaw
Author *sounds as if he is* ∧ <u>more correct</u> (6) = Writer.
  (A very rare example of having the ideal formulation –
  synonymcrux, fulcrum, keyword and exposition – slightly
  altered by putting the fulcrum where it isolates the exposition,
  not the synonymcrux.)
<u>Walk,</u> *say* /,\ **the Russian plain** (6) = Steppe
<u>Look again,</u> *say* /, at the\ **entertainment** (5) = Revue
<u>One</u> <u>resting on one's knees,</u> *say* /,\ **toughening metal** (9)
  = Annealing
<u>Czech, say,</u> <u>went first</u> /and\ **governed** (10) = Controlled
Names ∧ *said* to be used for <u>mountains</u> (12) = Appellations
The said <u>school members</u> /are in\ **the country** (5) = Wales
Not worth considering ∧ *the said* <u>fowls</u> (6) = Paltry
<u>One</u> *said to be* <u>without</u> ∧ **hairspray** (7) = Lacquer

Homophone (Keywords)

Prime time /for\ <u>making dried grass</u>, *so it might be said* (6)
   = Heyday
Girl /has\ <u>a</u> <u>large</u> <u>drink</u> *as stated* (7) = Abigail
<u>Girl</u> *reported to be with* <u>unpleasant</u> ∧ **line of rulers** (7) = Dynasty
Seeing /that\ <u>one is quoting</u> *aloud* (8) = Sighting
European flower /with\ *utterly* <u>distinctive smell</u> (4) = Oder
   (This must be one of the world's finest keywords ever! Utterly
   and flower are homographs, and Oder is a homophone.)

It is rare to find a homophone without a keyword, but there is an
exception to every rule.

<u>Took, without approval</u>, /that\ **French hat** (5) = Toque
<u>Country-dance</u> <u>period</u> /,\ the **prime of one's life** (6) = Heyday
<u>Unsophisticated</u> ∧ **Oriental novelist** (6) = Greene
As it may be <u>said</u>, <u>no</u> ∧ **good-looker** (6) = Adonis
   (The keyword in this clue is an anagram indicator, there is no
   homophone!)

STRUCTURE
The answer is always a synonym of the synonymcrux, never a
synonym of the exposition. The exposition is always synonymous
to the word that sounds like the answer. All the above examples
illustrate this fact. Furthermore, the tendency is for homophones
to adhere closely to the ideal structure of the cryptic clue, in spite
of exceptions. When the homophone has no synonymcrux it is
not much fun to solve the clue.

Pair of comedians might fire this? (10) = Cannonball
<u>Lusty</u> <u>animal</u> *reported* found roaming in S Africa (10) = Hartebeest

Humer

A humer is a type of crossword clue that involves humans directly. The humans are the subject matter of the clue. Humers are not, like most types of clue, concerned with method. The methods used in humers are dependent on the type of devices found in the humer.

As the clue types of straight clues were drawn into cryptic clues, so the cryptic clue types are drawn into the humer to be used as devices. Backwords, acronyms, anagrams, ammels, bridgewords, homophones and all the other types of clue will be found in the humer. Since humers are not a method of manipulating information to solve clues, the humer cannot be used as a device in other types of clue. Humers may be used in conjunction with other types of clue, as in the case of buildwords.

A humer is a type of crossword clue that involves humans directly. Probably far more than half of all clues involve humans in some indirect way.

Running the wrong way (11) = Mismanaging
Who runs? The almost full-grown maiden and her beau who grow old together (miss, man, aging)? Although the ellipsed human subject exists and occurs (almost) twice in the answer, this clue is not a humer. It would have been if miss, man and aging had featured in the clue.

At a guess:
At least one third of all crossword clues are full-grown humers.
In 80 per cent of humers the clue contains a name or an epithet in either the synonymcrux or the exposition.
In another 80 per cent of humers the answer contains either a name or an epithet.

And it is likely that:
Only 8 per cent of humers have a name or epithet in the clue only.

Humer

8 per cent of humers have a name or epithet in the answer only.
64 per cent of humers have a name or epithet in the answer and the clue.
20 per cent of humers have no name or epithet at all.
Different crosswords will show different distributions.

Epithet is used in its widest sense: Jack, the Redcoat, master carpenter, don, golfer, villager, German, womaniser, taximan, freshman, lip-reader, nipper, rival and the old church leader. How many of these epithets are gender biased? All of them, although golfer, master carpenter, villager, German, freshman, lip-reader, nipper, rival and the old church leader may be applied to any sex. It would be considered unsporting by many to advance beyond the old gender stereotypes and set clues in feminine terms.

Cheats /\ **music women?** (8) = Fiddlers
Newcomer /,\ **an inexperienced lass** (8) = Freshman
She /\ may be flagging in her duties (9) = Signaller
She lets loose /and is\ about to curse *badly* (7) = Rescuer
She /\ puts her arm into a sling (11) = Catapultier

Whether right or wrong, the tendency is that fewer than 20 per cent of humers involve women, and of those only about 20 per cent are epithets. Women's names feature prominently among the few female humers. But, at present, 80 per cent of humers remain distinctly masculine, which is a reflection of the implicit values words have. A shift in gender tendencies in other fields (e.g., employment and feminist thinking) will clearly lead to similar shifts in crosswords. Eventually.

The keywords to look for in spotting humers are the vocational suffix -er, other vocational suffixes, names and epithetic words, personal and possessive pronouns, man, girl, woman, family members and titles.

The remainder of this section does not require in-depth study.

Humer

THE VOCATIONAL SUFFIX, ESPECIALLY -ER

When the synonymcrux contains the vocational suffix -er, the answer is either an epithet or a famous name.

<u>A</u> <u>permit</u> *held by* <u>the</u> /\ **runner** (7) = Athlete
<u>Advances</u> /\ **a member of the family** (7) = Stepson
<u>Alternative</u> <u>number</u> *first by* /\ **a singer** (5) = Tenor
Amateur /\ <u>singer</u> = Layman
American beggar /–\ <u>a kitchen worker?</u> (10) = Panhandler
Amongst the ~~arrivals~~ /was\ the **challenger** (5) = Rival
As defier of the Conqueror /,\ <u>he</u> *takes* <u>the prize</u> (8) = Hereward
By <u>way</u> of <u>peak,</u> *following* <u>a</u> /\ **flyer** (7) = Aviator
Challenger /\ *from* ~~ched~~<u>dar</u> er~~adicated~~ (5) = Darer
<u>Cure a huff,</u> *doing a round* /,\ with **a driver?** (9) = Chauffeur
<u>Faultless</u> /\ **probationers?** (7) = Novices
Labourer /\ *gives* <u>vegetables</u> *to* <u>social worker</u> (7) = Peasant
Newcomer /,\ <u>an inexperienced chap</u> (8) = Freshman
<u>No</u> ~~record~~ *endlessly arranged* /for\ the **singer** (7) = Crooner
<u>Notice</u> <u>face protection</u> /for\ **teacher** (7) = Advisor
Offender /\ <u>cut lip</u> *badly* ~~right~~ *inside* (7) = Culprit
Radio buffs /make\ <u>poor players</u> (4) = Hams
<u>Word of impatience</u> <u>alternatively</u> /given by\ **teacher** (5) = Tutor
Ans~~wer~~ <u>wooden</u> /\ **old church leader** (6) = Anselm
As it may be <u>said, no</u> /\ **good-looker** (6) = Adonis
Composer /takes\ <u>girl</u> to <u>America</u> (6) = Lassus
Furniture designer /\ *to* <u>append</u> *adjustment in the* <u>country</u> (11) = Chippendale
<u>Lots irate</u> *about* /\ **an old philosopher** (9) = Aristotle
Maker of laws /\ <u>some</u> *break on* <u>Sunday</u>? (5) = Moses
Painter /\ <u>bamboozles</u> <u>board</u>! (9) = Constable
Painter /had\ *small* ho~~use~~ *with a* <u>courtyard</u> (7) = Hogarth
<u>Tuneful</u> /\ **American painter** (8) = Whistler

Humer (The vocational suffix, especially -er)

As is the case with the vocational suffix -er, all other vocational suffixes (-ist, -eer, -ant, -or, -nic, -ess, -ette, -man) and vocations generally in the synonymcrux lead to an epithet or a name (usually famous) in the answer.

Antagonist /\ these days raves *about* railway (9) = Adversary

Archdeacon *accepts* nearly ten /from\ **a spiteful woman** (5) = Vixen

Buccaneers /\ traipse *about* (7) = Pirates

Budding mathematician? (7,5) = Problem child

Col. Potter's calm *about* /being\ **a hobbyist** (5-9) = Stamp-collector

Declared as true /by\ **this accountant** (9) = Certified

Despot /\ has car *and rickety* cart (8) = Autocrat

Had eg *repeatedly confused* /\ **the intellectual** (7) = Egghead

Halfwit /\ finds it easy *to put* weight *on* (9) = Simpleton

I speak maliciously /about\ the **inhabitant** (8) = Islander

Incompetent /\ **worthy** (7) = **Not**able

Lousy actor /,\ gets this from critics? = Hammer

Made a move to train as /a\ **mechanic** (7) = Artisan

Mercenary /\ to engage the services of Heather (8) = Hire**ling**

Minor cleric /\ *needs* a little company *in the* study (6) = De**acon**

Nude *with* an *eccentric* /\ **governess!** (6) = Duenna

Pupils /\ of the past (6) = Alumni

Sailors /\ can, *in* tattered clothes (7) = Rati**ngs**

Sailors /\ *of the* Tsar (4) = Tars

The brain /behind\ smart denim *fashion* (10) = Mastermind

They'll put on /\ speculators (8) = Assumers

Tom, a thief who is extremely nimble (3-7) = Cat-burglar

Treason *perpetrated by* /\ **legislator** (7) = Senator

Trippers' coach? (7-6) = Dancing-master

Usherette /who's\ **a star** (7,4) = Leading lady

Confident-*sounding* /\ **dramatist** (4) = Shaw

Doubly evil **sailor** (6) = Sinbad

Sculptor /\ Ronald *embracing* Diana (5) = Rodin

Unsophisticated /\ **Oriental novelist** (6) = Greene

Welshman /\ provided alternative (4) = If**or**

Humer (The vocational suffix, especially -er)

When the vocational suffix, -er is found in the exposition, there is very often a partword in the answer that is a synonym of the -er word. A universal favourite is worker = ant.

A spinner at his /\ **peak?** (4) = **A**top
Auditor /perhaps\ hired Bill to tell the worker (9,10) =
    Chartered account**ant**
Coloured /\ worker *in* transport (7) = Sl**ant**ed
Officer *and* I make notes /\ **speaking in indefinite terms** (12)
    = **General**ising
Trippers' coach? (7-6) = Dancing-**master**

The same is true if any other epithet, with or without another vocational suffix (eg -or), is found in the exposition.

American sailors *first* /coming from\ **Paul's birthplace** (6) = **Tars**us
Author *on the* ri̶g̶h̶t̶ /\ **fence** (7) = **Barrie**r
Nurse *has* attempt at /finding\ **an animal** (5-4) = **Nanny**-goat
Offensive /\ rumour *about* a *retired* doctor (7) = Noi**som**e

The expositional epithet's synonym, the partword in the answer, is often a name.

Girl able *to recall* /\ **a whole lot of dates** (7) = **Alma**nac
Girl *having* a breather /on the\ **peak** (7) = **Ev**erest
Girl *reported to be with* unpleasant /\ **line of rulers** (7) = **Dy**nasty
Girl *without* a /\ **messenger** (5) = Angel (Angel**a**)
Girl's command /causes\ **confusion** (8) = **Di**sorder

The vocational suffix -er in the keyword is surprising. Leader abounds, but other vocational suffix -er keywords are extremely rare!

Ambassador /\ presents award *to* T̶o̶r̶y̶ *leader* (8) = Diploma**t**
Do not stand a r̶e̶v̶o̶l̶u̶t̶i̶o̶n̶a̶r̶y̶ *leader* /taking\ the **instrument** (5)
    = Sit**ar**

Humer (The vocational suffix, especially -er)

Gracious /\ ~~group~~ *leader is in the* <u>country</u> (6) = Be**nign**
<u>Help</u> ~~rebel~~ *leader first* /in\ **attack** (4) = **R**aid
<u>Hurried</u> *with* <u>Dutch</u> *leader's* /\ **currency** (4) = Rand
It is irregular /for\ ~~youth~~ *leader* <u>to make a grab</u> *first* (7) = Snatchy
<u>Left</u> *with* ~~revolutionary~~ *leader* /,\ **he is past recovery** (5) = Goner
Loot /for\ *lost, leaderless* ~~L~~ollards (7) = Dollars
<u>Prepared</u> *to include* <u>c</u>~~heer~~*leader in* /\ **the body of the followers** (4) = Sect
Quickly /\ <u>on top</u> *struggling to contain* <u>rebel</u> *leader* (6) = Pronto
<u>Resistance fighter</u> *with no leader* /is\ **a skilled worker** (7) = Artisan
To <u>every one</u> *the* ~~youth~~*-leader* /is\ **a friend** (4) = All**y**
~~Young~~ *leader* <u>Bill</u> *had* <u>night</u> *out* /\ **sailing** (8) = **Y**achting
Offered /\ *stranger* <u>a bed</u> (4) = Bade

Leader is seldom used other than to indicate an undix or addix (i.e., adding or removing letters) as above.

<u>Boast</u> *to* <u>ex-Labour leader</u> /proves\ **a bloomer** (8) = Crowfoot
Possibly the leader /will make\ <u>it clear</u> (7) = Article

The vocational suffix -er in the answer is clearly the consequence of an epithet or another vocational suffix in the synonymcrux.

American beggar /–\ **a kitchen worker?** (10) = Panhandler
Challenger /\ *from* ~~cheddar eradicated~~ (5) = Darer
<u>I speak maliciously</u> /about\ the **inhabitant** (8) = Islander
Lousy actor /,\ <u>gets this from critics?</u> = Hammer
<u>No recor</u>~~d~~ *endlessly arranged* /for\ the **singer** (7) = Crooner
Paid informer (12) = Schoolmaster
They'll put on /\ <u>speculators</u> (8) = Assumers
Trippers' coach? (7-6) = Dancing-master

NAME IN AN ANSWER
Humers with names are of two types: first names or famous names. Names are very seldom found in the synonymcrux. An epithet in the synonymcrux, it has been shown, yields a name (or epithet) in the answer.

Humer (Name in an answer)

FIRST NAMES
An Irishman ∧ apt *to be rebellious* (3) = Pat
Bit of a ~~problem~~ ma~~rrying~~ this ∧ **girl!** (4) = Emma
Di, the *curious* ∧ **lady** (5) = Edith
Diana's *replaced by another* ∧ **woman** (5) = Nadia
Eric *going wild about* the *French* ∧ **girl** (6) = Claire
First post ∧ lady? (5) = Penny
Girl ∧ *found in the* ~~cellar~~ (4) = Ella
Girl ∧ has a large drink *as stated* (7) = Abigail
Girl ∧ *models* are evil (7) = Valerie
He's ∧ *put* soldiers *back* ~~in-charge~~ (4) = Eric
Heather *dropping* a ∧ **boy** (4) = Eric
Her wager *is about* ~~right~~ /for\ **a man** (7) = Herbert
It's sweet and sticky /,\ **darling** (5) = Honey
Lady ∧ *removed* rich stain (9) = Christina
Little point in /being\ **a lady?** (3) = Dot
Looking slyly *at* cat /,\ **one that pries** (7,3) = Peeping Tom
Man ∧ *in a whirl* (4) = Eddy
Man ∧ is *back before* Mon~~day~~ (5) = Simon
Man ∧ makes appeal *to* energetic ~~royal~~ (6) = Oliver
Man /to\ ~~com~~pete readily *within* (5) = Peter
One real *disaster* /for\ a **girl** (7) = Eleanor
Pester ∧ him (5) = Harry
Scottish cattle ∧ man (5) = Angus
She ∧ gets the same bit of ~~luck~~ *twice* (4) = Lulu
The boy ∧ *to become* warden (6) = Andrew
Welshman ∧ provided alternative (4) = Ifor

FAMOUS NAMES
~~Answer~~ wooden ∧ **old church leader** (6) = Anselm
As it may be said, no ∧ **good-looker** (6) = Adonis
Can ∧ kid (5) = Billy
Confident-*sounding* ∧ **dramatist** (4) = Shaw
Dotty **type** (7) = Braille
Doubly evil ∧ **sailor** (6) = Sinbad
Furniture designer ∧ *to* append *adjustment in the* country (11)
    = Chippendale

Humer (Name in an answer)

Guided <u>a</u> /\ **Spartan queen** (4) = Leda
He /is\ *mentioned in passing in* ~~Samu~~el I~~V~~ (3) = Eli
H~~enry~~ <u>prepared to go</u> *in front* /of\ **the third son** (4) = Seth
<u>Jenny</u> /the\ **architect** (4) = Wren
John /of\ <u>Orange</u>? (4) = Peel
<u>Lots irate</u> *about* /\ **an old philosopher** (9) = Aristotle
Maker of laws /\ <u>some</u> *break on* S~~unday~~? (5) = Moses
~~Nothing~~ *less than* a <u>lifeless</u> /\ **deity** (5) = Woden
Painter /\ <u>bamboozles board</u>! (9) = Constable
Painter /had\ *small* ho~~use~~ *with a* <u>courtyard</u> (7) = Hogarth
Pair of comedians might fire this? (10) = Cannonball
Poet /\ <u>writes note</u> *held by disheartened* ~~si~~nger (7) = Spenser
Sculptor /\ <u>Ron</u>~~ald~~ *embracing* <u>Di</u>~~ana~~ (5) = Rodin
<u>Tuneful</u> /\ **American painter** (8) = Whistler
<u>Unsophisticated</u> /\ **Oriental novelist** (6) = Greene
Vacuum /left by\ <u>former FBI chief</u> (6) = Hoover
Wise old Greek /gets\ <u>emergency call</u> *about* <u>case</u> (8) = Socrates

NAME IN A CLUE

Any name in a clue is indicative of a need for specific letters in the answer. These letters may be taken by way of an anagram, a backword, an abbreviation or initial, a homophone or even a synonym of the name (Bill = Acc, Jack = AB = Tar, Sue = litigate, Edward = ted = ed). The most common use for a name is an anagram.

ANAGRAMS

<u>Col. Potter's calm</u> *about* /being\ **a hobbyist** (5-9) = Stamp-collector
<u>Erin paid out</u> *recklessly* /despite\ the **cancellation** (11)
   = Repudiation
<u>Evil Sue</u> *could be* /\ **difficult to pin down** (7) = Elusive
<u>Fay fell</u> *out* /\ **found at the end of the book** (7) = Flyleaf
Fruit /\ <u>in the scones Ruth</u> *prepared*! (5,8) = Horse chestnut
Fruit /\ <u>Irene can't</u> *remove* (9) = Nectarine
<u>Hampton's</u> *weird* /\ **ghost** (7) = Phantom
<u>Hat Annie</u> *removed* /from\ **one in Greece** (8) = Athenian
<u>Joan I'd</u> *moved* /\ **to be next to** (6) = Adjoin

Humer (Name in a clue)

Mass Caine *mutiny* is always new to **these people** (9)
   = Amnesiacs
Took away /from\ Ted, carted *off* (9) = Detracted

BUILDWORDS
Auditor /perhaps\ hired Bill to tell the worker (9,10) =
   Chartered accountant
Foreman ∧ to ignore Rex (8) = Overseer
From Missouri, Ronald /,\ a **feeble-minded person** (5) = Moron
Jack *with* a number of lines will ∧ **hang around** (5) = Tarry (Jack
   = Jack Tar, ry = abbreviation of railway = number of lines)
Nude /,\ *distracted,* hit Neal at the same time (2,3,10) =
   In the altogether
Tom *returns by* alternative /form of\ **transport** (5) = Motor

PRONOUNS – PERSONAL AND POSSESSIVE

'I' IN ANAGRAMS
Coming from port shop I /*made* for\ the **boat** (9) = Troopship
Deft clue I *manipulated* /*being*\ **crafty** (9) = Deceitful
Forceful ∧ chap I met *in trouble* (8) = Emphatic
Gnat I *disturbed* /was\ **a monster** (5) = Giant
I backed Ru *wrongly* /*producing*\ **a bloomer** (9) = Rudbeckia
I grasp one *form of* ∧ **foreign capital** (9) = Singapore
I meant *another* ∧ **person in an institution** (6) = Inmate
I praised *revolutionary* ∧ **Soviet committees** (8) = Presidia
I printed *out* /in\ **bold** (8) = Intrepid
Muslim ∧ claims I *sorted out* (7) = Islamic
Notorious ∧ gorge I use *by arrangement* (9) = Egregious
Plant ∧ parts I said *intertwine* (10) = Aspidistra
Porter *and* I *stumbled on* a ∧ **place in S Africa** (8) = Pretoria
Stagy way ∧ that Clare *and* I *performed* (10) = Theatrical
Things worth remembering ∧ I blame Mario *about* (11)
   = Memorabilia

Humer (Pronouns – personal and possessive)

'I' IN BUILDWORDS

'Vehicle I ~~had~~ *in the* house' /in\ **Japanese code** (7) = Bushido
After half-time, I ~~have~~ the right /\ **fur** (7) = Miniver (Half of Min~~ute~~)
Attack /\ animal, one I ~~left~~ (6) = Assail
But *in retreat* I ~~have~~ /to be\ **devious** (7) = Evasive
Con~~stance~~ *and* Den~~ise~~ *leave* /\ **make it briefer** (8) = Condense
English money I need *to change* /\ **in Holland** (6) = Leiden
Everybody, say, with alternative I state /\ **to be symbolic** (11)
    = Allegorical
Firm *has* no profit, I *conclude* /, from\ **huge statues** (7) = Colossi
Hearing /of\ examination I *take* on (8) = Audition
He~~nry~~ and I excel, *despite* /\ **disadvantage** (8) = Handicap
I draw *most of* the post *outside*, it's /\ **a condition of agreement**
    (11) = Stipulation (I, Station, pul~~l~~)
I *go in* to ward off /\ the **demon** (5) = Fiend
I swear it has been stained a **red colour** (6) = Bloody
I throw ~~nothing~~ *up* /,\ not even these **old coins** (5) = Oboli
In turn I /see\ the **film** (5) = Movie
It is clear *model and* I ~~have~~ /to be\ **mournful** (9) = Plaintive
Law I state /\ **of the words of language** (7) = Lexical
Officer *and* I make notes /\ **speaking in indefinite terms** (12)
    = Generalising
On *returning* I *take* part /in\ **offensive** (7) = Noisome
Remains *with* one I ~~left~~ /\ **found on the boat** (8) = Staysail
~~Right~~ *in* place *leave* /a\ **positive electron** (8) = Positron
Speaker *and* I ~~love~~ /\ **sacred music** (8) = Oratorio
Stan~~ley Church~~ *and* I operating the /\ **bar** (9) = Stanchion
State /\ '~~I love~~ Western-~~Australia~~' (4) = Iowa
Suit /\ I *found in* Ealing area (6) = action (Acton)
Vessel I ~~caught~~ /in\ **terror** (5) = Panic
Without initiative /, but\ I ~~have~~ *to* succeed *first* (7) = Passive

'I' IN A SPLITWORD AND A BRIDGEWORD

I speak maliciously *about the* **inhabitant** (8) = Islander
Wanting some ~~grub~~, I stro~~de~~ /into\ **cafe'** (6) = Bistro

'HE', 'HIM' AND 'HIS' IN THE SYNONYMCRUX

'He', 'him' and 'his', in the synonymcrux, yield an epithet in the answer.

<u>Additional</u> <u>Stock Exchange employee</u>, ∧ **he does casual work** (3-6) = Odd-jobber

Although of little value /,\ **he will <u>produce</u> <u>a burden</u>** (10) = Makeweight

<u>Another one might be set to catch</u> **him** (5) = Thief

Author ∧ *sounds as if* he is <u>more correct</u> (6) = Writer

<u>Before</u> *accepting* <u>discharge</u> /,\ **he was a recluse** (7) = Eremite

Disorganised <u>engineer</u> *involved in* <u>poor</u> work /but\ **he does produce a barrel** (6) = Cooper

Does **he** ∧ have some <u>degree</u> <u>with</u> <u>skills</u>? (6,2,4) = Master of arts

He ∧ <u>doesn't believe in anything fancy</u> (7) = Realist

He ∧ <u>doesn't get a place in the race</u> (4-3) = Also ran

He has been instructed to vote ∧ <u>for</u> <u>two unknowns</u> (5) = Proxy

He ∧ <u>has the star part in a western</u> (7) = Sheriff

He ∧ <u>illegally deprives another of a living</u> (8) = Murderer

<u>He is not accompanied</u> /by a\ **wild animal** (4) = Stag

He lets loose /and is\ <u>about</u> to <u>curse</u> *badly* (7) = Rescuer

He makes deals /with\ <u>many</u> <u>operating</u> <u>farm machinery</u> (10) = Contractor

He ∧ <u>may be flagging in his duties</u> (9) = Signaller

He ∧ <u>picks things up mechanically</u> (5-6) = Crane-driver

He ∧ <u>puts his arm into a sling</u> (11) = Catapultier

<u>He-helper</u>? (10) = Manservant

Of course ∧ **he's an expert** (7) = Tipster

<u>Officers find him revolting</u> (8) = Mutineer

<u>Once</u> <u>in the theatre</u> /,\ **he demands his moneyworth** (7) = Exactor

Pester ∧ <u>him</u> (5) = Harry

'HE', 'HIM' AND 'HIS' IN THE EXPOSITION

In the exposition 'he', 'him' and 'his' function as bitwords. They are often addixed (add a dix) into an answer. When this happens 'he' does not necessarily indicate an epithet in the answer.

He *has* a fish /for\ **curing** (7) = Healing
He re~~ally~~ *lost his* friend /\ **at this place** (4) = Here
He's a lot /on\ **edge** (3) = Hem
He's *going* round again /\ **in this area**! (10) = Hereabouts
As defier of the Conqueror /,\ he *takes* the prize (8) = Hereward

'SHE' AND 'HER' EPITHETICALLY IN THE SYNONYMCRUX
Does **she** tend to work in her own area? (8,5) = District nurse
Don't hit /\ **her** (4) = Miss
She /\ gets the same bit of lu~~ck~~ *twice* (4) = Lulu
She nurtures young /\ lepidopterist! (6) = Mother

AS A BITWORD IN THE EXPOSITION
Her wager *is about* r~~ight~~ /for\ **a man** (7) = Herbert
Practical joker /has\ ~~n~~o tool *in* her ~~possession~~ (6) = Hoaxer

BY EXCEPTION, AS FULCRUM
Strangely hag los~~t~~ *most of* /her\ **shoe**! (6) = Galosh

'THEY' AND 'THEIR'
'They' and 'their' occur epithetically, usually in the synonymcrux.

They gave a skilful performance /,\ but caused our visit *to be rescheduled* (8) = Virtuosi
They'll put on /\ speculators (8) = Assumers
They'll /\ support the board (8) = Trestles
They're /\ needled, and respond to pressure, naturally (10) = Barometers
They're /\ settled collectively in Israel (9) = Kibbutzim

PERSONAL NOUNS

MAN IN THE SYNONYMCRUX
In the synonymcrux man becomes epithetic by inclusion in compounds; Irishman, nobleman, countryman, churchman, German. In any event, if man is in the synonymcrux, the answer holds either a name or an epithet.

A serving man ∧ *once* <u>raced to</u> *serve* (7) = Redcoat
A skilful man, ∧ <u>does he teach woodwork?</u> (6,9) = Master carpenter
An Irishman ∧ <u>apt</u> *to be rebellious* (3) = Pat
<u>Assume it is</u> ∧ a **Spanish nobleman** (3) = Don
Cheats ∧ **music men?** (8) = Fiddlers
<u>Clever fellow</u> *and a* <u>soldier</u> *are both* ∧ **wise men** (4) = Magi
Clubman (6) = Golfer
Countryman ∧ *has* <u>drink</u> *after* <u>6.50</u> (8) = Villager
Foreman ∧ <u>to ignore</u> R~~ex~~ (8) = Overseer
Her <u>wager</u> *is about* r~~ight~~ /for\ **a man** (7) = Herbert
<u>Laird can</u> *become* ∧ **a high churchman** (8) = Cardinal
Man ∧ <u>in a whirl</u> (4) = Eddy
Man ∧ <u>is</u> *back before* Mon~~day~~ (5) = Simon
Man /makes\ <u>appeal</u> to <u>energetic</u> r~~oyal~~ (6) = Oliver
Man /to\ ~~com~~<u>pete readily</u> *within* (5) = Peter
Mark<u>s**man**</u>? (6) = German
<u>Night-watch</u>**man!** (10) = Astronomer
<u>Norma wise</u> *about* ∧ **ladies' man** (9) = Womaniser
Scottish cattle ∧ <u>man</u> (5) = Angus
Spanish nobleman ∧ <u>concealed</u> <u>gaol</u>*break* (7) = Hidalgo
Welshman ∧ <u>provided</u> <u>alternative</u> (4) = Ifor

MEN IN THE EXPOSITION
In the exposition there is a tendency for the answer to contain a
synonym of man.

<u>A male</u> ∧ **go-between** (5) = A**gent**
Check development ∧ <u>of this man taking actor's place</u> (5) = Stunt
Cleaner ∧ <u>to put</u> a <u>man</u> <u>off</u> (9) = Deter**gent**
<u>Man</u> *accepting* <u>alternative</u> ∧ **spirit** (6) = **M**orale
North American ∧ <u>may, these days,</u> *accompany* <u>a Scottish man</u>
   (8) = Cana**dian**
<u>One</u> *held by* <u>Spanish man</u> ∧ **of high rank** (6) = **Senior**
<u>Wise men</u> <u>about</u> *to produce* ∧ **some tricks** (5) = **Mag**ic

When man occurs in the answer it is usually epithetic, being part
of a compound.

4. Nonconstruction-type Clues

Humer (Personal nouns)

Among ~~them another~~ ∧ **virile fellow** (2-3) = He-man
<u>Duty charged</u> *on one* <u>fellow</u> ∧ **driver** (7) = Taximan
He-helper? (10) = Manservant
<u>Information</u> <u>let</u> *out by* <u>one person</u> /,\ **male** (9) = Gentleman
Newcomer /,\ <u>an inexperienced chap</u> (8) = Freshman
<u>Poet</u> *or* <u>teacher</u> *perhaps* ∧ **found on the football field** (8) = Linesman

'GIRL', 'WOMAN' AND 'LADY' IN THE SYNONYMCRUX
Be late /for\ **girl** (4) = Miss
Bit of a ~~problem~~ <u>marrying</u> this ∧ **girl!** (4) = Emma
<u>Eric</u> *going wild about* <u>the</u> *French* ∧ **girl** (6) = Claire
Girl ∧ *found in the* ~~cellar~~ (4) = Ella
Girl /has\ <u>a</u> <u>large</u> <u>drink</u> *as stated* (7) = Abigail
Girl ∧ *models* <u>are evil</u> (7) = Valerie
<u>One real</u> *disaster* /for\ a **girl** (7) = Eleanor
<u>Di, the</u> *curious* ∧ **lady** (5) = Edith
Does she tend to work in her own area? (8,5) = District Nurse
<u>Don't hit</u> ∧ **her** (4) = Miss
<u>Equipment</u> *returned* and ~~left~~ *with the* ∧ **young lady** (4) = Girl
First post ∧ <u>lady?</u> (5) = Penny
Foreign ladies /with\ <u>sons are</u> *affected* (7) = Senoras
Lady ∧ *removed* <u>rich stain</u> (9) = Christina
<u>Little point</u> in /being\ **a lady?** (3) = Dot
Noble lady /is\ <u>unrivalled</u>, *but without* <u>money</u> (7) = Peeress
<u>Archdeacon</u> *accepts* <u>nearly ten</u> /from\ **a spiteful woman** (5) = Vixen
Chesswoman? (5) = Queen
<u>Diana</u>'s *replaced by another* ∧ **woman** (5) = Nadia

'GIRL', 'WOMAN' AND 'LADY' IN THE EXPOSITION
There is a tendency for the answer to contain a synonym for woman.

Composer /takes\ <u>girl</u> to <u>America</u> (6) = **Lass**us
<u>Girl</u> <u>able</u> *to recall* ∧ **a whole lot of dates** (7) = **Almanac**
<u>Girl</u> *having* <u>a breather</u> /on the\ **peak** (7) = **Ever**est
<u>Girl</u> *reported to be with* <u>unpleasant</u> ∧ **line of rulers** (7) = **Dyna**sty
<u>Girl</u> *without* <u>a</u> ∧ **messenger** (5) = **Angel**
<u>Girl's</u> <u>command</u> /causes\ **confusion** (8) = **Dis**order

WOMEN IN THE ANSWER AS A SYNONYM OF THE SYNONYMCRUX

Archdeacon *accepts* nearly ten /from\ **a spiteful woman** (5) = Vixen
Be late /for\ **girl** (4) = Miss
Chesswoman? (5) = Queen
Equipment *returned* and ~~left~~ *with* the ∧ **young lady** (4) = Girl
Foreign ladies /with\ sons are *affected* (7) = Senoras
Indian nurse ∧ *from* ~~Bombay~~ – a ~~hard~~ worker (4) = Ayah
Noble lady /is\ unrivalled, *but without* money (7) = Peeress
   (~~Peer~~less L stands for pounds in Lsd)
Nude *with* an *eccentric* ∧ **governess!** (6) = Duenna
She nurtures young ∧ lepidopterist! (6) = Mother
Usherette ∧ who's a star (7,4) = Leading lady

WOMEN AS A SYNONYM OF THE EXPOSITION

Commonsense /or\ parental humour (6-3) = **Mother**-wit
Composer /takes\ girl to America (6) = **Lass**us
Imagine ∧ mother *going round* again (5) = **D**ream
Kill mother /from\ **some land** (6) = Domain
Letter from Greece ∧ is *sent up with* a note *to* mother (5) = Sig**ma**
Mother's *turn* /to\ **stifle** (7) = **S**mother
Mum *goes round* a mark left /by\ **make-up** (7) = **M**ascar**a**
Nude *with* an *eccentric* ∧ **governess!** (6) = **D**uen**na**
Nurse *has* attempt at /finding\ **an animal** (5-4) = **N**anny-goat

PERSON OR CHILD IN THE SYNONYMCRUX

A person or child in the synonymcrux leads to an epithet in the answer.

A person facing the truth ∧ about a heel (7) = Realist
An individual ∧ seeing what others have to say (3-6) = Lip-reader
Corset – an *essential* /for\ **the older person** (8) = Ancestor
Drinks /for\ **kids** (4) = Tots
Information let *out by* one person /,\ **male** (9) = Gentleman
Thievish ∧ **child?** (6) = Nipper
Wordy *exchange* /from\ **disorderly person** (5) = Rowdy

4. Nonconstruction-type Clues

Humer (Personal nouns)

'ONE'

'One' in the synonymcrux, used epithetically, leads to an epithet in the answer.

Champion debtor /,\ **one who confers gifts** (8) = Bestower
Go round *with* a garment /for\ **one who has changed sides** (8)
   = Turncoat
One contributing /to\ *performance of* rondo (5) = Donor
One /\ drawing the less serious side of life (10) = Cartoonist
One /\ finding it amusing in a silly way presumably (7) = Giggler
One follows /\ smash-hit *with* operational-research (9) = Successor
One frequenting /\ a section Hugh *is said to have gone round* (7)
   = Habitué
One /\ having nine tenths of the law (9) = Possessor
One /is\ barely recognisable out of gear (6) = Nudist
One /\ may be caught out (9) = Cricketer
One of the best artistes (4) = Star
One paid to work /in\ tavern's *restoration* (7) = Servant
One /\ taking stock of others (7) = Rustler
One /\ under-employed (4-6) = Mine-worker
One using a sound device /\ *puzzling* punters (7) = Punster
One who hits out /–\ at a blackleg? (7) = Striker
One who is against /\ work *has a* problem (7) = Opposer
One /\ who is dear but not near (6,6) = Absent friend
One who overpraises /\ even more so *with* hesitation (9) =
Flatterer (flat, flatter, er)
One who persistently annoys /\ *another* ganger (6) = Nagger

'ONE' IN EXPOSITION USED EPITHETICALLY

Another one might be set to catch /\ **him** (5) = Thief
Caught *by* one with an inclination /to become\ a **char** (7) = Cleaner
He /\ draws when one is open-mouthed (7) = Dentist
Number /\ one /\ specialist (6) = Egoist
One cannot go straight ahead /and make\ **it** (6) = Detour
One has a job to eat in /\ **it** (5,7) = Works canteen
One is put out when shown **this** (4) = Door
One may peg out /playing\ **it** (7) = Croquet (Croak it)

144

One of the family *takes* the <u>veil</u> /in\ **religious order** (11) = Brotherhood
One *said to be* <u>without</u> /\ **hairspray** (7) = Lacquer
One <u>saying it</u> /is\ **an old Greek coin** (6) = Stater
One <u>up</u> /with an\ **amendment** (5) = Rider

'ONE' USED AS 'A'
Japanese warrior /\ *is* imbibing <u>a</u> <u>drink,</u> <u>one</u> *knocked back* (7)
   = Samurai (is = Si, drink = rum, a = a, one = a, a rum
   'knocked back' = mura)
One <u>donated</u> /\ an **American aloe** (5) = **A**gave
One *getting in the* <u>shed</u> *about* <u>to regret</u> /\ **the arrogance** (7)
   = Hauteur
One ~~needs to~~ <u>get</u> *round* <u>a</u> *hidden* /\ **stone** (5) = **A**gate
One <u>resting on one's knees,</u> *say* /,\ **toughening metal** (9)
   = **A**nnealing
One <u>unwell</u> *during the* <u>poetry</u> /at\ **the château** (10) = Versailles

'ONE' USED AS 'I'
<u>Duty charged</u> *on* <u>one</u> <u>fellow</u> /\ **driver** (7) = Taximan
One <u>about</u> *to contain* <u>tribal</u> *warfare* /is\ **easily annoyed** (9)
   = Irritable
One, *before* <u>nine,</u> *taking in* <u>a</u> <u>novice</u> /\ **who is queuing up** (2,1,4)
   = In a line
One <u>fled</u> /\ the **country** (4) = Iran
One *held by* <u>Spanish man</u> /\ **of high rank** (6) = Senior
One <u>member</u> *with wrong* <u>deed</u> /was\ **hindered** (7) = Impeded

'ONE' AS 'UN' IN FRANCE
The obvious keyword makes this device easy to spot.

One *from France* <u>ruined</u> /\ **what was natural** (8) = **Un**spoilt
One *in France* <u>keeled over</u> /as it was\ **ex-directory** (8) = **Un**listed
One *in France* <u>to bring in</u> <u>worker</u> /–\ **how trifling** (11) =
   Unimportant
One *in France,* <u>it</u> /is\ **one** (4) = **Un**it
One *Parisian in the* <u>p~~a~~rk</u> /,\ **a follower of aggressive rock music** (4)
   = Punk

Humer (Personal nouns)

'ONE' IN AN ANAGRAM

All the short numbers are often used as bitwords to be included in other words.

One isn't *creating* ∧ **a state of suspense** (7) = Tension
One *maybe* according to reason ∧ **concerned with new works**
  (10) = Neological
One real *disaster* /for\ a **girl** (7) = Eleanor

'ONE' IN AN UNDIX

~~One appreciated~~ *part of* ∧ **the smallest range of tides** (4) = **Neap**
~~Penny~~ *had less than* one quarrel /with\ **the high priest** (7) = Pontiff

ODD ONE, ONE THING OR ANOTHER

An instrument /one needs\ to fix *in* place (6) = **Spin**et (pin in set)
One ∧ buys things in Barcelona (6) = Peseta
One in seven /is\ *from* ~~men vying for top jobs~~ (4) = Envy
  (Envy is one of the 'seven deadly sins'.)
One of the toasts ∧ that may be offered with a meal (7) = Crouton
One ∧ *piece of* ~~amm~~unition (4) = Unit

FATHER AND MOTHER

Father and mother are almost always parabrebitted to Ma and Pa or Pop and Dam. The resultant bitwords are stacked in the answer. It goes without saying that father and mother are not likely to be found in the synonymcrux.

Attract ∧ father *bringing up* ring (6) = **Ap**peal
Father *finds* ~~an~~ animal *back* /at\ the **temple** (6) = **Pa**goda
Father *going by* luxury car /has\ **fish** (4) = **Pa**rr
Father ~~right~~ *to* accept /and\ **participate** (7) = **Parta**ke
Pop *back* for the painting /,\ **separately** (5) = **Ap**art
Remarkable detail Pop *produced, without* hesitation /,\ **of**
  butterflies and moths (11) = Lepidoptera
Single-parent child /,\ but left shares *in profusion* (10) = Fatherless
Common sense /or\ parental humour (6-3) = **Mother**-wit
Imagine ∧ mother *going round* again (5) = **Dream**

<u>Kill mother</u> /for\ **some land** (6) = Do**ma**in
Letter from Greece /\ <u>is</u> *sent up with* <u>a note</u> *to* <u>mother</u> (5) = Sig**ma**
<u>Mother's</u> *turn* /to\ **stifle** (7) = **Smother**
<u>Mum</u> *goes round* <u>a</u> <u>mark left</u> /by\ **make-up** (7) = **Ma**scara
She nurtures young /\ <u>lepidopterist!</u> (6) = **Mother**

RANK OR TITLE
This is usually an indicator of a humer with an epithet in the answer.

A serving man /\ *once* <u>raced to</u> *serve* (7) = Redcoat
Ambassador /\ presents <u>award</u> *to* ~~Tory~~ *leader* (8) = Diplomat
<u>Assume it is</u> /\ a **Spanish nobleman** (3) = Don
Chesswoman? (5) = Queen
Despot /\ *has* <u>car</u> *and rickety* <u>cart</u> (8) = Autocrat
<u>Guided a</u> /\ **Spartan queen** (4) = Leda
Labourer /\ *gives* <u>vegetables</u> *to* <u>social worker</u> (7) = Peasant
<u>Laird can</u> *become* /\ **a high churchman** (8) = Cardinal
Minor cleric /\ *needs* <u>a</u> *little* <u>~~company~~</u> *in the* <u>study</u> (6) = Deacon
Noble lady /is\ <u>unrivalled</u>, *but without* <u>money</u> (7) = Peeress
<u>Officer</u> *and* <u>I</u> <u>make notes</u> /\ **speaking in indefinite terms** (12)
    = Generalising
<u>One</u> *held by* <u>Spanish man</u> /\ **of high rank** (6) = Senior
Spanish nobleman /\ <u>concealed</u> *gaolbreak* (7) = Hidalgo
Trouble /\ <u>has</u> *surrounded* <u>Abyssinian prince</u> (6) = Ha**rass**

ANIMALS, BIRDS AND FISH
Usually part of a genus and specie device

Cattle fodder /from\ **Northern Europe** (5) = Swede
<u>Disputatious</u> /\ **turtles?** (11) = Loggerheads
<u>Drink</u> ~~left~~ /for\ **a bird** (4) = Teal
Duck down (5) = Eider
Fish /\ *in the* ~~shop a hake~~? (4) = Opah
Fish /or\ <u>cut grass</u> *round* <u>hotel</u> (6) = Minnow
King /\ <u>penguin?</u> (7) = Emperor
<u>None</u> *over* <u>ten</u> <u>look at</u> /\ this **flower** (2-3) = Ox-eye

Humer (Personal nouns)

Nurse *has* <u>attempt</u> <u>at</u> /finding\ **an animal** (5-4) = Nanny-goat
<u>Spaniel</u> *with* <u>the</u> *Spanish* ∧ **bird** (8) = Cockerel
Untidy ∧ <u>little creature?</u> (6-3) = Litter-bug
Beast ∧ *has* ~~nothing~~ *in the* <u>pub</u> (4) = Boar
Bird ∧ *moves out of* <u>danger</u> (6) = Gander
<u>Bird</u> *not* ~~to~~ *come up* /for\ **fish** (4) = Parr (parrot)
Bird /or\ <u>fish</u> <u>a pig</u> *consumed* (7) = Sparrow
<u>Bird</u> <u>pecked</u> ∧ **a morsel** (6) = Titbit
Bird ∧ <u>seen while others retreat</u> (4) = Skua
<u>Bird</u> <u>to irritate</u> ~~right~~ ∧ **beetle** (10) = Cockchafer
Birds ∧ <u>model</u> *it* *in the* <u>football team</u> (8) = Bluetits
<u>Brazilian footballer</u> *on the way up* <u>has</u> *included* <u>book</u> /of\ **large animals** (9) = Elephants
Brush ∧ <u>plant</u> (5) = Broom

THE ABUSE OF THE -ER VOCATIONAL SUFFIX
Propeller ∧ <u>operating back to front</u> (7) = Oarsman
<u>Boast</u> *to* <u>ex-Labour leader</u> /proves\ **a bloomer** (8) = Crowfoot
<u>Dispute</u> *after* <u>dispute</u> /for\ the **winger** (7) = Sparrow
How some <u>waiters</u> ∧ **formed a line** (6,2) = Queued Up
<u>I backed Ru</u> *wrongly* /producing\ a **bloomer** (9) = Rudbeckia
<u>Nora</u> *Batty* /,\ **flower of Italy?** (4) = Arno

& Lit

The & Lit clue is a clue of another type and literally true, too. A clue that is merely literally true is not an & Lit; & Lits must be cryptic in structure too.

<u>Tersest</u> **testers** (7) = Setters (Coherent anagram & Lit)
Some ∧ ~~nasty~~ <u>eye</u> ∧ **infection** (4) = Stye (Bridgeword & Lit)
Stocking a ship /with\ <u>cargo</u> (6) = Lading (Extended synonymtwin & Lit)
<u>Washington</u>, **say** (5) = State (Synonymtwin & Lit)
Last ∧ <u>but two to score</u> (10) = Eighteenth (Extended synonymtwin & Lit)
It ∧ <u>is the language!</u> (7) = Italian (Extended synonymtwin & Lit)

Put ∧ *head of* ~~department~~ **in** clue (7) = Include (Condix & Lit)
When <u>Ian's aorta</u> *ruptured* he went into ∧ **one of these** (9)
   = Sanatoria (Anagram & Lit)
Tear <u>Alec</u> **to pieces** (8) = Lacerate (Anagram & Lit)
One *of the* ~~best artistes~~ (4) = Star (Bridgeword & Lit)

Here are some clues that may or may not be & Lit clues.
<u>**Highlight**</u> of 70s fashion trousers? (5) = Flare
Asked /for\ <u>breakfast</u> *in* <u>bed?</u> (6) = B**egg**ed (Concon & Lit?)
<u>**Storm**</u> on stage (7) = Tempest (Classical allusion & Lit?)
Changing <u>at noon</u> (8) = **Am**ending (Splitword & Lit?)

Nosek

The nosek is a type of clue which has **No S**ynonymcrux,
Exposition or **K**eyword.

Usually this type of clue involves a 'very clever pun' that often fails
to amuse the solver. The structure of the clue should not be
sacrificed for the sake of a pun or a joke, since the lack of structure
can ruin the beauty of the joke. (The sections on palindromes and
phrases will illustrate how well good puns an be used in well
structured clues.) Fortunately the nosek is not excessively used,
since it seems too much like a straight clue.

Apparently senseless communication (9) = Telepathy
Cheeky, but attractive, features (7) = Dimples
Clubman (6) = Golfer
Domestic storm centre (6) = Teacup
Falsified one's accounts? (4) = Lied
Forger's block (5) = Anvil
In orbit, one looks out (7) = Eyeball
Mainly susceptible to heavenly attraction (5) = Tidal
No man's land taken over by Napoleon (6,4) = Animal Farm
Not a friendly state (6) = Enmity
Officers find him revolting (8) = Mutineer
One may peg out playing it (7) = Croquet

Nosek

Plate of fish? (5) = Scale

They're needled, and respond to pressure, naturally (10)
    = Barometers

This lighting is very bad! (5) = Arson

Triangle on a potter's table? (5) = Frame

Typical finishing stroke (5) = Serif

When bulbs come to life? (4) = Dusk

Dotty type (7) = Braille

Bank of Scotland (4) = Brae

Queue outside a baker's shop? (9) = Breadline

Stern guide (6) = Rudder

Thievish child? (6) = Nipper

'And Thou beside me singing . . .' (Omar Khayyam) (2,3,10) =
    In the wilderness

'Man is by nature a political -. . .' (Aristotle) (6) = Animal

Its passengers don't take flight (4) = Lift

It depends on the listener (7) = Earring

It needs another three, just the same as this, to make a circle (8)
    = Quadrant

It assists the diver to go up rather than down (11) = Springboard

It is used for making cuts in the theatre (8,5) = Surgeon's knife

Is the sitting room the place for this seat? (7) = Lounger

Is one unable to find any apples or bananas in it? (9,6) =
    Fruitless search

Is this how a flaming row was started? (7,3) = Sparked off

Is this where one might see acts of violence? (7,2,3) =
    Theatre of war

Is it eaten for high-tea? (5-4) = Tipsy-cake

Is there something less than honest in the manufacture of
    sunglasses? (5,8) = Shady business

Phrase

A phrase is indicated by the num of the clue when the num contains more than one number. The numbers will be separated by commas or hyphens. A comma indicates separate words, each having the number of letters indicated. A hyphen in the num means that a hyphen occurs in the answer after and before the specified number of letters.

Much inferior /being\ <u>in another part of town perhaps</u> (3,2,3,4,6)
    = Not in the same street
Very easy to understand ∧ <u>in the fortune-teller's sphere</u> (2,5,2,7)
    = As clear as crystal
We run until we <u>drop</u> /in this\ **race** (3-3-5) = Egg-and-spoon
<u>Neat</u> ∧ **barrier** ∧ **on the way** (6-4) = Cattle-grid

Hyphens and commas do occur in the same num.

Even this <u>express</u> must come to a <u>halt</u> eventually (3-4,5) =
    Non-stop train

Apostrophes, like hyphens and spaces, are not assigned a square of their own, nor are they ever indicated in any way.

Light /,\ <u>charmed object able to grant all one's desires</u> (8,4) =
    Aladdin's lamp (written aladdinslamp in the puzzle)

Phrases are generally quite easy to solve, but nonetheless involve a wide variety of devices in their solution.

Stacking paraphrased words is the most common practice in clueing phrases.

<u>Neat</u> ∧ **barrier** ∧ **on the way** (6-4) = Cattle-grid
<u>No cost</u> *to the* <u>worker</u> /for this\ **drawing** (4-4) = Free-hand
<u>Stupid</u> <u>attendant</u> /in the\ **lift** (4,6) = Dumb waiter
<u>Pining,</u> <u>about to put on</u> ∧ **a record** (4-7) = Long-playing

Phrase

Recorded ∧ <u>having filched</u> <u>a</u> duvet (4,4) = Took down
Tired /of\ <u>everything</u> <u>trendy</u> (3,2) = All in
<u>Blend</u> <u>wine</u> *first* /producing\ a **fungicide!** (8,7) = Burgundy mixture
Manage somehow /to\ <u>produce</u> *and* <u>act</u> (4,2) = Make do

There is very often something of the Debono (involving lateral thinking) in the phrase clue.

<u>Restarting</u> the crossword (4,2,6,3) = Back to square one
Birth certificate? (8,4) = Delivery note
Feline ∧ coming to an abrupt end (4,3) = Manx cat
Simple task /,\ <u>piloting a prairie schooner?</u> (5,7) = Plain sailing

EXTENDED SYNONYMTWIN
Resolute ∧ <u>drama students are</u> (8,2,3) = Prepared to act
Honestly /it is\ <u>without curves and climbing</u> (8,2) = Straight up
<u>Au fait with recent changes</u> ∧ **until now** (2,2,4) = Up to date
Sign indicating <u>where road works usually are</u> /–\ **in front** (5)
   = Ahead

HUMER
<u>Looking slyly at</u> <u>cat</u> /,\ **one that pries** (7,3) = Peeping Tom
Not in the majority (5,3) = Under age
Still in the minority (5,3) = Under age
A skilful man /,\ <u>does he teach woodwork?</u> (6,9) = Master carpenter
<u>Charge</u> <u>Bill</u> /hopes\ **this will be refunded** (7,7) = Expense account
<u>Understand</u> <u>revolutionary</u> /will become\ **furious** (3,3) = See red
Server <u>who is speechless?</u> (4-6) = Dumb-waiter
<u>Notice</u> <u>politician</u>'s ∧ **departure from text** (2,3) = Ad lib

NOSEK
Tranquil waters? (7,5) = Pacific Ocean
<u>Flaming</u> <u>practice!</u> (4-5) = Fire-drill
Series of local calls (3-5) = Pub-crawl
Even this <u>express</u> must come to a <u>halt</u> eventually (3-4,5) =
   Non-stop train
Vehicle one might jump on? (9) = Bandwagon

ANAGRAM IN EXPOSITION

Is content with present achievements /,\ <u>reason nurse let loss</u>
  deteriorate (5,2,4,7) = Rests on one's laurels

Successful people in it *suffering* <u>total non-reality?</u> (8,7) =
  National lottery

ANTONYMIC EXPOSITION

Don't remain <u>wholly</u> calm (2,2,6) = Go to pieces

Destined ∧ *never* to be in good health? (3-5) = Ill-fated

<u>Get off</u> /or\ **put on the line** (4,2) = Hang up

A BACKWORD IN THE EXPOSITION

Determined ∧ *the* <u>records</u> *should be brought up* (3,2) = Set on

CONDIX IN EXPOSITION

Deputise /for\ <u>n̶e̶w̶-̶d̶e̶p̶u̶t̶y̶-head</u> *in* <u>disgrace</u> (5,2) = Sta**nd** in

ELLIPSIS

We run until we <u>drop</u> in this **race** (3-3-5) = Egg-and-spoon
  (We run until we drop **the egg** in this race, not until we
  ourselves drop down exhausted.)

TAUTOLOGY

See ∧ *double* (2,3,6) = Lo and behold

Doubly <u>evil</u> ∧ **sailor** (6) = Sin**bad**

PLEONASM

How <u>one</u> plays cards ∧ **alone?** (6-8) = Single-handedly

GENUS AND SPECIE

We run until we <u>drop</u> /in this\ **race** (3-3-5) = Egg-and-spoon

Quotation

'And thou beside me singing . . .' (Omar Khayyam) (2,3,10) =
    In the wilderness
'Man is by nature a political . . .' (Aristotle) (6) = Animal

Synonymtwin (homograph)

> Synonymtwins are not synonyms of each other but are related
> to one another by virtue of having a common synonym. The
> different meanings of a single homograph are synonymtwins
> of one another.

A thesaurus lists the synonyms of the headword in a lemma,
consequently the listed synonyms of the headword are all
synonymtwins of one other. The homograph 'right', for example,
includes these synonyms: honest, true, square, straight,
auspicious, sane, starboard, Tory, obverse, unmitigated, licence,
integrity, well. The synonyms of 'right' (or any given word) are
synonymtwins of each other.

The synonymtwin, when referring to a type of cryptic crossword
clue, is strictly a two-word clue, of which the two words are
synonymtwins of each other and synonyms of the homographic
answer. The structure of the clue is a dead give-away of its type.

The best synonymtwins contain a pasop. This means that one is
misled by the apparent part of speech where the words of the clue
seem to modify the meaning of one another. They do not: the two
words must be read in isolation, or each in relation to the answer.

Lean ∧ <u>over</u> (5) = Spare
Kind ∧ <u>face</u> (4) = Type
<u>Conspicuous</u> ∧ **gesture** (6) = Signal
Stay ∧ <u>second</u> (7) = Support
General ∧ <u>allowance</u> (5) = Grant

Leaves /\ <u>cracks</u> (4) = Goes
Rich /\ <u>wit</u> (5) = Comic
<u>Blackish</u> /\ **wharf?** (5) = Jetty
Tidy /\ <u>stock</u> (4) = Neat
Assemble /\ <u>fitting</u> (4) = Meet
Pleasantly /\ <u>subtle</u> (4) = Nice
European /\ <u>perch</u> (4) = Pole
<u>Devilishly</u> /\ **infer?** (5) = Imply
<u>Watch</u> /,\ **say** (7) = Observe
African /\ <u>wasteland</u> (4) = Moor

Sometimes the synonymtwin may contain a fulcrum word, which, according to the purists, makes it an extended synonymtwin.

Keep /the\ <u>jam</u> (8) = Preserve
Bargain /for\ <u>crop</u> (4) = Snip
<u>Shoot</u> /and\ **wound** (5) = Spear
Port /and\ <u>orange</u> (5) = Jaffa

Extended synonymtwin

> An extended synonymtwin is a synonymtwin of more than two words.

Prying person /receives\ <u>a severe rebuff</u> (5) = Noser
Staunch /\ <u>supporter of a flower</u> (4) = Stem
<u>Do not leave</u> /\ **shore** (4) = Stay
American beggar /–\ <u>a kitchen worker?</u> (10) = Panhandler
<u>Appear intelligent?</u> /\ **Be quick** (4,5) = Look sharp

Look out for the fulcrums, being and for and their equivalents.

An individual who minds /being\ <u>sensitive</u> (6) = Tender
Bear /to be\ <u>a Hindu ascetic!</u> (4) = Yogi
Bargain /for\ <u>crop</u> (4) = Snip
Be late /for\ <u>girl</u> (4) = Miss
<u>Drinks</u> /for\ **kids** (4) = Tots

Extended synonymtwin

<u>Prize</u> /is a\ **handle!** (5) = Lever
<u>Visit briefly</u> /to make\ **an inspection** (4,4) = Look into

The extended synonymtwin, which effectively has a double synonymcrux, is a great favourite for defining answers that are phrases.

To be successful ∧ <u>produce the article yourself</u> (4,2) = Make it
Make friends ∧ <u>do a quick repair job</u> (5,2,2) = Patch it up
Where <u>a gangway seat</u> /is\ **ultimately correct** (5,2,3,3) =
    Right at the end
Finished ∧ <u>covering the whole lot</u> (3,4) = All over
Abandon demand /to\ <u>descend</u> (5,4) = Climb down
Making some progress /, though\ <u>plainly ageing</u> (7,2) = Getting on
Delay /caused by\ <u>armed robbery</u> (4,2) = Hold up
Free of debt /and\ <u>held in esteem</u> (2,6) = In credit
<u>Available to customers</u> /, or\ **about to arrive** (2,5) = In store
Attack ∧ <u>a lazy loafer</u> (3,5) = Lay about
Lower /when\ <u>disappointed</u> (3,4) = Let down
<u>Where to put the acne ointment</u> ∧ **at once?** (2,3,4) = On the spot
Vigilant ∧ <u>like the eyes of a time-keeper</u> (2,3,5) = On the watch
Just what is needed /,\ <u>padding?</u> (5,3,5) = That's the stuff
Ayes /for\ <u>the blue-eyed boys</u> (5,2,6) = Those in favour
Initiate /with\ <u>the gun mechanism ready</u> (7,3) = Trigger off
Given instructions ∧ <u>as monks are</u> (5,6) = Under orders

Look out for the irony of antonymic (of opposite meaning) clues.

Keeps going /, or\ <u>waits</u> (5,2) = Hangs on
Containing the most subject-matter /but\ <u>of least interest to a
    vegetarian</u> (8) = Meatiest

The Final Word:
A Caveat

The (putative) rules described in this book must very clearly be seen as flexible and changing with gradually fading peripheries rather than being rigid and clearly defined. They are conventions, not rules. Exceptions abound to such an extent that they eventually become conventions themselves. Victorian anagrams were used, by exception, as part anagrams, giving rise to beheadments and curtailments, then to disheartenments, to caudations and finally to dixes. Each exception to the rule is justified in its familial resemblance to the existing body of rules, conventions and accepted clues. New conventions resemble the old ones more or less, as children resemble their parents and the game of crosswords lives and propagates itself through rebellious descendants. And through them too, the game lives.

PART FOUR

Appendix

Comparative table of differences and similarities in nomenclature of segments or word parts

Segment*	Dix (& Dixeme)	Affix	Grapheme	Morpheme	Phoneme	Syllable	Bitword	Partword
Definition	A meaningless piece of a word taken from a word to make a new word. (beST ARtist)	An addition or element placed before, in or after the body or root of a word to modify its meaning.	The smallest whole unit of writing that has lexical meaning; (e.g. a letter, not a jot, tittle or serif).	The smallest meaningful structural unit that is an element of a word. (Di-phthong/	The smallest unit of sound in writing. (Ph, f, sh, o, oo)	A unit of pronunciation uttered without interruption or pause. (Diph-thong)	**A whole word** of less than four letters.	A whole word that exists inside of other words. (e.g., not in an**other**)
Makes … Made of …	Dixes make new words. Made of pieces of words.	Makes new meaning in a word. Made of graphemes and phonemes.	Makes words and all word parts. Made of symbolic lines and dots.	Makes words. Made of graphemes and phonemes.	Makes syllables. Made of graphemes.	Makes words. Made of graphemes and phonemes.	Makes twords, if used with dixemes and words. Made of syllables, graphemes, morphemes.	Partwords make answers for crosswords. Made of pieces of words.
Like Unlike	Like affix, grapheme, morpheme, phoneme and syllable. Unlike them in function.	Like morphemes and syllables in appearance, at times. Unlike in function.	Like phonemes in appearance, at times. Unlike in function.	Like syllables in appearance, at times. Unlike in function.	Like graphemes (and digraphs) in appearance. Unlike graphemes in function.	Like morphemes and affixes in appearance at times. Unlike in function.	Like syllables. Unlike any part because of being a whole word.	Like words in appearance. Unlike dixes.
Form	No fixed form.	A large range of fixed forms.	A small range of fixed forms.	A vast range of regular forms.	A few regular forms.	A vast range of regular forms.	A vast range of regular forms.	Fixed forms of regular words.
Meaning	Has no own, intended meaning.	Has its own consistent meaning.	Has no meaning.	Has meaning, in context.	Has no meaning.	Has meaning, in a whole word.	Has its own, intended meaning.	Has its own, intended meaning.

Segment*	Dix (& Dixeme)	Affix	Grapheme	Morpheme	Phoneme	Syllable	Bitword	Partword
Influence on meaning	The dix does not amend the meaning of a word. It radically alters the word so that it bears no relation to the baseword. The dix makes new words.	It amends meaning, not of a word, but its context (number, tense, gender, part of speech, etc).	Graphemic symbols convey meaning in context of words or abbreviations.	Have own meaning, modified by conjunction with other morphemes.	When used in recognised patterns the patterns have meaning.	Affects the meaning of adjacent syllables when in whole words.	Affects the meaning of adjacent words when in collocations, sentences, or phrases.	The partword does not amend the meaning of its host word. Its presence is purely accidental.
Application	Relevant to two words only, in the context of one crossword clue.	Regularly applied to all of a class of word stems.	Regularly applied with each other in set patterns.	Regularly applied with each other in set patterns.	Regularly applied with each other in set patterns.	Regularly applied with each other in set patterns.	Regularly used in sentences, phrases and collocations.	Relevant in situ only, in the context of a word game.
Function	Has no grammatical or conventional lexical function.	Has a grammatical function.	Has a regular lexical function.	Has a regular lexical and syntactic function.	Has a regular lexical function.	Has a regular lexical function.	Has a regular grammatical and lexical function.	Has no grammatical or conventional lexical function.
Species of the genus	Undix: Removing part of a word. Addix: Appending part of a word.	Divided into three categories: prefix, infix and suffix.	Alphabets and writing signs. (e.g., '?-I a +)	Very many, divided by syntactic and grammatical function.	Many, divided by sounds in words.	Very many, divided by function in words.	Very many, by spelling.	None.

*A phonetics and linguistics term for any discrete, physically or auditorily identifiable speech unit.

Glossary

This glossary includes words used in the text and other words that are relevant to word games generally.

abbreviation, n.	1. Word or phrase shortened to initials or a meaningful part thereof. 2. Crossword device used to reduce the number of letters in the exposition, especially common in straight clues and in buildwords.
across, adj.	Written from left to right, as answers are in lights of a crossword.
acronym, n.	Word or name made of the stacked initials of a phrase.
ammel, n.	1. Crossword clue where the headword of a dictionary lemma is the answer and its definition is the clue, e.g., Organ stop with string tone (5) = Gamba. Includes synonyms (Bog-myrtle (4) = Gale) and genus-and-specie clues (Tree (5) = Maple). 2. Crossword device where the definition of a lemma is part of the exposition. [f. lemma, backwards]
anagram, n.	A word or phrase made by transposition of letters of another word or phrase, e.g., Nastier = ratines, resiant, restain, retains, retinas, retsina, stainer, starnie, stearin, earns it, in tears, it's near, nears it, nits are, sin rate, sit near, snare it, stare in, tins are, etc.

andor, conj.	And and or or or or and. Meaning both or either of the two words ('And **and** or') or ('or **or** and'), e.g., 'The options are peanut butter andor jelly. Sometimes written as and/or.
answer, n.	1. Response. 2. Solution to a problem. 3. Solution in response to a crossword clue.
antonym, n.	Word of contrary meaning to another, e.g., High or low; the opposite of synonym.
apostrophe, n.	1. Sign of elision or possessive case. 2. In crosswords, often a key to an anagram or an answer using the same letters, e.g., Kindergar<u>ten 'e ment</u>ioned in flat (8) = Tenement.
backword, n.	Word that, when reversed, forms a new word, but not a palindrome, e.g., repel = leper, warts = straw.
barred diagram, n.	Crossword grid devoid of blanks, where the end of each light is indicated by a bold line.
baseword, n.	Word that can be changed by adding a dix to make a word with a word inside it (a tword), e.g., Two + rd = tword (baseword + dix = tword).
beheadment, n.	Removal of the initial letter of a word which leaves the remainder of the original word as a new word itself, e.g., Blooming, looming; Flatter, latter; flight, light.

bitword, n.	1. Word of less than four letters. 2. In crosswords, an abbreviation of less than four letters of a word or phrase. (See parabrebit.)
blank, n.	Black square in a crossword grid, i.e., neither unch nor rech.
blocked diagram	Crossword grid.
bridgeword, n.	1. Hidden word formed by the last part of the first word and the first part of the last word of consecutive words. The bridgeword may include a partword, e.g., Some drago**ons laugh,** taking fierce attack = Onslaught. 2. Crossword device that employs a bridgeword in the exposition. 3. Type of crossword clue using bridgeword in exposition, e.g., **Of odd origin**, /but\ w**hy bridg**eword? (6)= Hybrid. (f. Bridge across words.)
buildword, n.	Type of crossword clue where the answer is formed by stacking words andor dixes from the exposition or a paraphrase thereof. The composition of the buildword may employ other crossword devices.
caudation, n.	Insertion of a letter at the end of a word; opposite of curtailment.
checked square, n.	A rech, or square common to two lights of a crossword.

clue, n, v.	1. Brief coded text understood by cognoscenti only. 2. Fact of statement or existence that suggests a line of thought enabling the discovery of a correct solution to a puzzle.
cognate anagram, n.	One of an anagram pair of related meaning, e.g., Angered = enraged; Astronaut = unto a star.
coherent anagram, n.	One of a number of adjacent anagrams used with coherent sense within a phrase or sentence, e.g., Palest pastel; Cheap peach; One's nose; Pirates traipse to parties.
compound word, n.	Single word made from two or more other words. e.g., bedroom or ballcock.
compound, n.	Description of a single concept or thing, expressed or named by more than one word, often hyphenated. e.g., Adam's apple; Full stop; No trump.
concatenate, v.	Join things together in series like the links of a chain.
concon, n.	Crossword device in which one word contains another to form a third word, e.g., rag + tin = ra**tin**g. (**Con**traction of **con**tainer and **con**tents)
concord, n.	1. Agreement in grammar between words in gender, number, tense, etc. 2. Agreement in crosswords between parts of answer and parts of clue, of words in gender, number, tense, part of speech, etc.

condix, n.	Container and contents word where either the container or the content (or both) is a dix instead of a word, e.g., Straggling (String containing a gg and l).
consonant, n.	Any letter of the alphabet, barring vowels (a, e, i, o, u, and sometimes y, as in fly).
contraction, v. or n.	1. Shrinking of a word or words by combination or elision. (v.) 2. Contracted word, e.g., She had = she'd; Forecastle = fo'c'sle. (n.)
crossletter, n.	Letter in a rech.
crossword, n.	Puzzle of language and skill in a chequered grid of crossing lights (across and down) which are filled by solving the given clues.
crux, n.	At the heart of something, the epicentre where all parts meet. (Latin – 'cross'.)
cryptic, adj.	1. Secret, mystical; containing a hidden meaning beyond the face value of the words. 2. Encoded so as to be deciphered by cognoscenti only. 3. Verbally brief, pithy.
cryptic clue, n.	1. Crossword clue that employs any number of recognised devices and usually has an exposition, a keyword and a synonymcrux. 2. Crossword clue other than a straight clue.

curtailment, n.	Removal of the last letter of a word which leaves the remainder of the original word as a new word itself, e.g., Fine, fin; Glade, glad; Lather, lathe; Planet, plane.
deletion, n.	Omission of part of a text; in crosswords usually part of a word.
device, n.	1. Literary stylistic verbal form or figure of speech used to give more value to words than their mere face value, e.g., irony, litotes, sarcasm, metaphor. 2. Stylistic verbal form used to give more value to words than their mere face value, e.g., anagram, macaroni, reversal, parabrebit, abbreviation, condix, homophone, pasop, splitword, stacking, partbit.
dictionary, n.	'A malevolent literary device for cramping the growth of a language and making it hard and inelastic. The present dictionary, however, is one of the most useful works its author, Dr John Satan, has ever produced. It is designed to be a compendium of everything that is known up to date of its completion, and will drive a screw, repair a red wagon or apply for a divorce. It is a good substitute for measles, and will make rats come out of their holes to die. It is a dead shot for worms, and children cry for it.' (From *The Enlarged Devil's Dictionary by Ambrose Bierce*, p 96).
digraph, n.	Two letters that represent a single sound, e.g., sh and ea in sheaf.

diphthong, n.	Combination of vowels to produce new sounds, e.g., ay, ou, ai, io.
dix, n.	Constructive unit of which words are built in word games, though not necessarily the smallest possible unit.
dixeme, n.	Minimal constructive unit of which words are built in word games and the central concern of dixology.
down, adj.	Written from top to bottom, as answers are in lights of a crossword.
elision, n.	1. Omission of vowel or syllable in pronouncing, marked by apostrophe when written. 2. Crossword device indicating that the letters near the apostrophe in the clue are used in the answer.
ellipsis, n.	Omission from sentence of words needed to complete construction or sense.
exposition, n.	1. Explanatory statement or account; an explanation or commentary. 2. Part of a crossword clue that explains the answer or confirms the correct synonym for the synonymcrux.
extended synonymtwin	Crossword clue that is a synonymtwin of more than two words. e.g., Consent to go (5) = Leave.

finisher (crossword finisher), n.	Finisher is a list of words sorted alphabetically in order of each letter of the word in turn (i.e., first sorted by the first letter, then sorted by the second letter, then the third letter, so that an alphabetic list is made of words having, for example, t in the third place), with a secondary ordering of another letter. These lists are made specifically to use crossletters as the source of the answer.
fulcrum, n.	1. Point on which a seesaw balances, or a lever is supported or turns. 2. Point or word in a cryptic crossword clue that separates the two definitions (exposition and synonymcrux) of the answer.
genus and specie	1. Crossword device that uses a genus in the exposition and a specie in the answer, e.g., <u>Heather</u>, *after* <u>a game</u>, **calling the dog** (9) = **Whist**ling. 2. Ammel using genus as clue and specie as answer, e.g., Heather (4) = Ling.
geograph, n.	Device in which solving clues depends on some geographical information or knowledge.
grapheme, n.	Smallest whole unit of writing that has lexical meaning, e.g., a letter, not a jot, tittle or serif.
grid, n.	Chequered square of (blanks, unches and reches or) crossing lights (across and down) which are filled by solving the given clues of a crossword.

halph, n.	A clue in which only half of a phrase is given and the other half is needed to construct the answer (a contraction of **Half** a **ph**rase).
hendiadys, n.	Expression of an idea by using two nouns instead of a word modifying another, e.g., nice and warm instead of nicely warm.
hidden word, n.	Plainly visible whole word that is concealed within the words of a cryptic crossword clue. The hidden word is usually the answer to the clue, but is sometimes merely a vehicle for finding the answer. The genus of hidden words is divided into several species, but mainly partwords, bridgewords, splitwords and backwords. Acronyms and anagrams are not hidden words because the answer is not seen as a whole word in the clue.
homograph, n.	Word spelled like another but with a different meaning or pronunciation, e.g., pig = **sow** = plant.
homonym, n.	Word of the same spelling and pronunciation as another but a different sense or meaning, e.g., tent **pole** or magnetic **pole**.
homophone, n.	Word pronounced like another, but with a different spelling and meaning. e.g., By, buy, bye; So sew; No, know.
humer, n.	Crossword device where the clue is indicative of the answer being some type of human, most often vocational. (f. **Hum**an with vocational suffix, **er**.)

hydration, n.	Insertion of a letter at the head of a word; opposite of beheadment.
insertion, n.	1. Act or an instance of inserting. 2. Amendment inserted into a text or into a word. 3. Addition of letters into a word in order to make a new word.
isolano, n.	Word that will not admit even a single letter-change, e.g., gnu, its, ova, urn, use.
jargon, n.	Words or phrases, and the meaning thereof, peculiar to a specific subject.
keyword, n.	1. Key to a cipher, etc. 2. Word of great significance. 3. Word or phrase that unlocks the meaning of the exposition of a cryptic crossword clue by revealing how its parts should be manipulated. The keyword plainly indicates the devices used in the exposition.
letter-change, n.	Deletion of a letter from a word with the insertion of a letter at the same place to make another word, e.g., Share – shore.
light, n.	1. Space for the whole answer of a crossword clue, formed of squares. 2. Sometimes, the answer of a crossword clue. 3. Rarely, the individual letters in the answer.
nosek	Clue that has no clear or discernible synonymcrux, exposition and keyword.

num, n.	Bracketed numeral of a crossword clue that indicates the number of letters required for each word of the answer, and hyphenation needed.
numer, n.	Crossword device that exploits verbal associations with numbers, or where symbols are both alphabetic and numeric and the ambiguity allows a solution of the clue.
olapsek, n.	Clue in which there is an <u>o</u>ver<u>lap</u> of the <u>s</u>ynonymcrux, <u>e</u>xposition and <u>k</u>eyword, e.g., *Some* ~~nasty eye~~ **infection** (4) = Stye (Bridgeword & Lit); One *of the* ~~best artistes~~ (4) = Star (Bridgeword & Lit).
onalosi, n.	Word of which any letter can be letter-changed, e.g., Shore and c, t, a, n, t, respectively to become chore, store, share, shone and short.
palindrome, n.	Word or series of words of symmetrical letter order, reversible letter by letter without any change other than the points of division between words, e.g., Madam, a man – a plan – a canal. Panama, madam.
parabrebit, n, v.	Crossword device used in buildwords to paraphrase and abbreviate (a word, phrase or exposition) to a bitword, e.g., <u>In</u>~~side~~ <u>archaeological excavation</u>, ~~name~~ <u>worker</u> ∧ **with scorn** = in dig n ant. (f. **Para**phrase and ab**bre**viate to **bit**word.)

paraphrase, v.	Express meaning of (passage or text) in other words.
parataxis, n.	Positioning of phrases andor clauses without conjunctions or other words to show their relationship, e.g., 'A man, a plan, a canal, Panama!' i.e., A man who had a plan to build a canal which came to be named Panama. Parataxis makes the palindrome possible.
paronomasia, n.	Pun.
paronym, n.	1. Word cognate with another. 2. Word formed from a foreign word.
part of speech, n.	Grammatical types of words, e.g., adjective, adverb, conjunction, interjection, noun, preposition, pronoun, verb.
partbit, n.	Part of a word which is undixed to build a new word. e.g., **Constellation** seen in the *second half of J*u*ly, the middle of Ma*r*ch and the first of A*pril* (4) = Lyra.
partword, n.	1. Hidden word wholly contained by another word, e.g., Laugh in on**slaugh**t; valid in compound words, e.g., bed in bedroom. 2. Crossword device that uses a partword in the exposition. 3. Type of crossword clue using a partword as exposition.
pasop, n.	Crossword device where **p**arts **of s**peech and **p**unctuation are deliberately confused in order to mislead. (f. Reversed acronym – **P**art **O**f **S**peech **A**nd **P**unctuation.)

phrase, n.	1. Few words customarily grouped together, often idiomatically. 2. In crosswords likewise, but including compounds.
pleonasm, n.	Needless repetition without synonyms of a defining property of a word, e.g., a round circle, a loud noise, divide into four quarters. Compare 'suddenly the balloon burst' to 'gradually the balloon burst', where the pleonasm is deliberately used for dramatic effect. Pleonasms frequently occur between the synonymcrux and the exposition of a clue. (See tautology.)
prefix, n.	Word or syllable added to the front of a word to amend its meaning.
pun, n.	Figure of speech that uses a deliberate ambiguity caused by the use of homophones or homonyms, most often to be funny.
rech, n.	Square common to two lights of a crossword, a checked square. (See Unch.) (f. Bridgeword in square, checked.)
reversal, n.	Creation of a word or dix from a series of letters which is read backwards, e.g., Grebe in iceberg.
splitword, n.	1. Crossword device where a series of letters may be split ambiguously, e.g., sing, listen. sin, glisten. 2. Words so formed, splitwords.

	3. Type of crossword clue using a splitword as exposition or answer, e.g., <u>Encourages a boy</u> to make **a side dish** (3,5) = Egg salad.
stacking, n, v, tr.	Crossword device where letters, bitwords and basewords are arranged in serial to make a word. The order of stacking is assumed front to back unless a keyword indicates otherwise. (f. Stacking kids' letter blocks.)
suffix, n.	Word or syllable added to the end of a word to amend its meaning.
synonym, n.	Word meaning the same as another word, but possibly suitable to a different context, e.g., picture, painting and portrait.
synonymcrux, n.	That part of a crossword clue that is a synonym of the answer and the crux of the clue. It is usually distinct from the exposition and keywords. It is set apart from the rest of the clue by a fulcrum.
synonymtwin, n.	Crossword clue of two words only, where both are synonymous to the answer, but not to each other. e.g., **Lean** over (5) = spare. (f. Twins by relation to answer.) An extended synonymtwin has more than two words, e.g., **Consent** to go (5) = Leave.
tautology, n.	Needless repetition of synonyms. e.g., Say it <u>over again once more</u>. (Repeat it again is a pleonasm because repeat means say it again but repeat and again are not synonyms.) In clues the synonymcrux and the exposition are often tautological.

transdeletion, n.	Deletion of a single letter from a word which is followed by the transposition of the remaining letters; an anagram of a word, less one letter, e.g., <u>Retail</u>, alter.
transinsertion, n	Insertion of a single letter to a word which is followed by the transposition of the new letters; an anagram of a word, plus one new letter, e.g., Groan + j = Jargon.
tword, n.	Word that contains a partword. Its remainder may be another partword andor a dix, or two dixes(tword rhymes with sword), e.g., **partword** contains pa, par, part, art, two tword, word or. (f. <u>Two word</u>s in one.)
unch, n.	Square peculiar to one light of a crossword; an unchecked square. See rech. [f. Partword in square, <u>unch</u>ecked.)
undix, n.	Crossword device where a dix is extracted from a tword or word to leave a baseword or bitwords suitable for use in the answer, or to be used in the answer itself, e.g., <u>Cha~~rles t~~he</u> *heartless* was /\ **sexually virtuous** (6) = Chaste.
word ladder, n.	Unbranched series of words, each letter-changed from its predecessor. Lewis Carroll called them 'doublets'.
word network, n.	Set of words related by letter-changes that is a branched word ladder.

Acknowledgements

This book was written partly in a psychiatric hospital, partly on the computers provided for us homeless people by charities in London, and partly on the computers of my friends Jacques and Lorraine.

Kindest thanks to Mrs Pringle, who wrote the introduction and did a great deal of the spadework in the preparation of this book at Stellenbosch during 1998 and 1999. Thanks also for for the use of computers or facilities and very kind assistance and support of the staff at the Town Library of Stellenbosch, the J S Gerike Library at the University of Stellenbosch, Stikland Hospital (Cape Town); and in London: The British Library, St Mungo's and Bridge Training Centre, The Passage, The Big Issue, All Saints' Church Carnegie Street, Union Chapel Homelessness Project, The Ace of Clubs, London Guildhall University and Lorraine Williams especially. Thanks to the editors, notably Eileen Jarvis, and to everyone at Foulsham for their expert help, patience and support. Thanks to John Hayward for permission to use the picture of me on the back cover. Thanks to Barry Belasco and Graham Kitchen, both at Foulsham, who treated me and my disability with kindness and tolerance; to Father Shaun Lennard, whose God empowers him; to Malcolm Nurick, without whose compassion and financial support the Hiddencode.co.uk would not have existed; and to Tanya, at Tyser Greenwood. Thanks to Felicity Mitchell at Merril Lynch for service beyond the call of duty. I find it appalling that more people are omitted from this page than are mentioned. It's terrible how I forget those who helped me. Thanks to Uncle Caspar, Lize, Yvette, Jacques, Mignon, Willie Goedvolk (who read Steinbeck to us), Pieter Kriel and Fiona, Gillian, Sister Cara Iosa and her sister nuns, Lorraine, Michael Potton, the Distillers of Laphroig, the Winemakers of the Cape and many other friends too numerous to mention who helped and supported me and tolerated my eccentricity and the madness of mental illness while I wrote this book. It means that those who love me stood by me.

Bibliography

This bibliography has been compiled to acknowledge, with sincere gratitude, the sources of information consulted while writing this book, and quoted or referred to in this book.

Magazines and Newspapers

Cook, Denise, 'Essentially Blocked', *Essentials*, December 1996, Republican Press, Mobeni, South Africa.

Fergusson, James, 'How to do *The Times* Crossword', *Mensa Quest*, April 1998. Pageant Publishing, London.

Mullins, Gerald, 'The blockword No 38', *Essentials*, June 1998, Republican Press, Mobeni, South Africa.

WH Crossword, *Sunday Times Magazine*, Times Media Ltd, Johannesburg. (By syndication. Copyright: *The Daily Telegraph* and *Sunday Telegraph,* London, 1996, 1997, 1998 and 1999.)

'Everyone's Crossword' 1996, 1997, 1998, 1999, *Sunday Times Magazine*, Times Media Ltd, Johannesburg (By syndication from the *Express*. Copyright © Peter Chamberlain/Express Syndication).

'2-Speed Crossword', *Sunday Times Magazine*, Times Media Ltd, Johannesburg.

The Telegraph 518, Friday 19 February 1999, *The Cape Times,* Independent Newspapers Holdings Ltd, Johannesburg.

'Take-a-break No 7200', *The Argus*, 24 September 1998, Independent Newspapers Holdings Ltd, Johannesburg.

Books

Allen, R E (Ed), 1990, *The Concise Oxford Dictionary of Current English (Eighth Edition)*, Clarendon Press, Oxford.

Augarde, Tony, 1984, *The Oxford Guide to Word Games*, Oxford University Press, Oxford.

Bailie, J M (Ed), 1992, *The Hamlyn Crossword Dictionary*, Chancellor Press, London.

Benson, Morton; Benson, Evelyn; Ilson, Robert; 1986, *Lexicographic Description of English*, John Benjamins Publishing Company, Amsterdam.

Benson, Morton; Benson, Evelyn; Ilson, Robert, 1986, *The BBI Combinatory Dictionary of English*, John Benjamins Publishing Company, Amsterdam.

Brewer, E Cobham, *The Dictionary of Phrase and Fable*, Galley Press.

Cowie, Anthony (Ed), 1992, *Oxford Advanced Learner's Dictionary of Current English (Fourth Edition)*, Oxford University Press, Oxford.

Crystal, David, 1985, *A Dictionary of Linguistics and Phonetics*, Basil Blackwell Ltd, Cambridge.

Curl, Michael, 1995, *The Wordsworth Dictionary of Anagrams*, Wordsworth Editions Ltd, Ware.

Daintith, John, 1993, *Anagram Finder*, Bloomsbury Publishing Ltd, London.

Dunwoody, Jack, 1994, *The Penguin Guide to Cryptic Crosswords*, Penguin Books, London.

Eckler, Ross, 1996, *Making the Alphabet Dance: Recreational Wordplay*, St Martin's Press, New York.

Griffiths, John, 1994, *The Cassell Crossword Finisher*, Cassell Publishers Ltd, London.

Hobbs, James B, 1986, *Homophones and Homographs*, McFarland, Jefferson.

Hopkins, Ernest Jerome (Ed), 1967, *The Enlarged Devil's Dictionary by Ambrose Bierce*, Penguin, London.

Howard-Williams, Jeremy, 1997, *The Complete Crossword Companion*, Harper Collins Publishers, London.

Manley, Don, 1992, *Chambers Crossword Guide*, Chancellor Press, London.

Newby, Peter, 1983, *Pears Word-Puzzlers Dictionary*, Pelham Books, London.

Pulsford, Norman G, 1967, *The Modern Crossword Dictionary*, Pan Books Ltd, London.

Stibbs, Anne (Ed), 1994, *Crossword Lists And Solver*, Bloomsbury Publishing Ltd, London.

Wells, David, 1987, *The Penguin Dictionary of Curious and Interesting Numbers*, Penguin Books, London.

Index

Bold in this index indicates the headword of an entry; brackets a definition.

Index

Personal Notes